OF MICE
AND MEN

John Steinbeck

SPARK PUBLISHING

122 Fifth Avenue
New York, NY 10011
www.sparknotes.com

ISBN 978-1-4114-6980-8

Please submit changes or report errors to www.sparknotes.com/errors.

Printed in Canada

10 9 8 7 6 5 4 3 2

CONTENTS

CONTEXT   I

PLOT OVERVIEW   5

CHARACTER LIST   9

ANALYSIS OF MAJOR CHARACTERS   I3
    LENNIE   I3
    GEORGE   I3
    CANDY   I4
    CURLEY'S WIFE   I5
    CROOKS   I5

THEMES, MOTIFS & SYMBOLS   I7
    THE PREDATORY NATURE OF HUMAN EXISTENCE   I7
    FRATERNITY AND THE IDEALIZED MALE FRIENDSHIP   I7
    THE IMPOSSIBILITY OF THE AMERICAN DREAM   I8
    THE CORRUPTING POWER OF WOMEN   I9
    LONELINESS AND COMPANIONSHIP   I9
    STRENGTH AND WEAKNESS   20
    GEORGE AND LENNIE'S FARM   20
    LENNIE'S PUPPY   20
    CANDY'S DOG   2I

SUMMARY & ANALYSIS   22
    SECTION I   22
    SECTION 2   25
    SECTION 3   29
    SECTION 4   32
    SECTION 5   36
    SECTION 6   38

IMPORTANT QUOTATIONS EXPLAINED   4I

KEY FACTS   47

STUDY QUESTIONS   49

HOW TO WRITE LITERARY ANALYSIS   51
    THE LITERARY ESSAY: A STEP-BY-STEP GUIDE   51
    SUGGESTED ESSAY TOPICS   63
    A+ STUDENT ESSAY   64
    GLOSSARY OF LITERARY TERMS   66
    A NOTE ON PLAGIARISM   68

REVIEW & RESOURCES   69
    QUIZ   69
    SUGGESTIONS FOR FURTHER READING   75

CONTEXT

JOHN STEINBECK WAS BORN IN 1902 in Salinas, California, a region that became the setting for much of his fiction, including *Of Mice and Men*. As a teenager, he spent his summers working as a hired hand on neighboring ranches, where his experiences of rural California and its people impressed him deeply. In 1919, he enrolled at Stanford University, where he studied intermittently for the next six years before finally leaving without having earned a degree. For the next five years, he worked as a reporter and then as caretaker for a Lake Tahoe estate while he completed his first novel, an adventure story called *Cup of Gold*, which was published in 1929. Critical and commercial success did not come for another six years, when *Tortilla Flat* was published in 1935, at which point Steinbeck was finally able to support himself entirely with his writing.

In his acceptance speech for the 1962 Nobel Prize in literature, Steinbeck said:

> . . . the writer is delegated to declare and to celebrate
> man's proven capacity for greatness of heart and
> spirit—for gallantry in defeat, for courage, compassion
> and love. In the endless war against weakness and
> despair, these are the bright rally flags of hope and
> of emulation. I hold that a writer who does not
> passionately believe in the perfectibility of man has no
> dedication nor any membership in literature.

Steinbeck's best-known works deal intimately with the plight of desperately poor California wanderers, who, despite the cruelty of their circumstances, often triumph spiritually. Always politically involved, Steinbeck followed *Tortilla Flat* with three novels about the plight of the California laboring class, beginning with *In Dubious Battle* in 1936. *Of Mice and Men* followed in 1937, and *The Grapes of Wrath* won the 1940 Pulitzer Prize and became Steinbeck's most famous novel. Steinbeck sets *Of Mice and Men* against the backdrop of Depression-era America. The economic conditions of the time victimized workers like George and Lennie, whose quest for land was thwarted by cruel and powerful forces beyond their control, but whose tragedy was marked, ultimately, by steadfast compassion and love.

Critical opinions of Steinbeck's work have always been mixed. Both stylistically and in his emphasis on manhood and male relationships, which figure heavily in *Of Mice and Men*, Steinbeck was strongly influenced by his contemporary, Ernest Hemingway. Even though Steinbeck was hailed as a great author in the 1930s and 1940s, and won the Nobel Prize for literature in 1962, many critics have faulted his works for being superficial, sentimental, and overly moralistic. Though *Of Mice and Men* is regarded by some as his greatest achievement, many critics argue that it suffers from one-dimensional characters and an excessively deterministic plot, which renders the lesson of the novel more important than the people in it.

Steinbeck continued writing throughout the 1940s and 1950s. He went to Europe during World War II, then worked in Hollywood both as a filmmaker and a scriptwriter for such movies as *Viva Zapata!* (1950). His important later works include *East of Eden* (1952), a sprawling family saga set in California, and *Travels with Charley* (1962), a journalistic account of his tour of America. He died in New York City in 1968.

THE HISTORY OF MIGRANT FARMERS IN CALIFORNIA

After World War I, economic and ecological forces brought many rural poor and migrant agricultural workers from the Great Plains states, such as Oklahoma, Texas, and Kansas, to California. Following World War I, a recession led to a drop in the market price of farm crops, which meant that farmers were forced to produce more goods in order to earn the same amount of money. To meet this demand for increased productivity, many farmers bought more land and invested in expensive agricultural equipment, which plunged them into debt. The stock market crash of 1929 only made matters worse. Banks were forced to foreclose on mortgages and collect debts. Unable to pay their creditors, many farmers lost their property and were forced to find other work. But doing so proved very difficult, since the nation's unemployment rate had skyrocketed, peaking at nearly twenty-five percent in 1933.

The increase in farming activity across the Great Plains states caused the precious soil to erode. This erosion, coupled with a seven-year drought that began in 1931, turned once fertile grasslands into a desertlike region known as the Dust Bowl. Hundreds of thousands of farmers packed up their families and few belongings, and headed for California, which, for numerous reasons, seemed like a promised land. Migrant workers came to be known as Okies, for although they came from many states across the Great Plains, twenty percent of the farmers were originally from Oklahoma. Okies were often met with scorn by California farmers and natives, which only made their dislocation and poverty even more unpleasant.

John Steinbeck immortalized the plight of one such family, the Joads, in his most famous novel, *The Grapes of Wrath.* In several of his fiction works, including *Of Mice and Men,* Steinbeck illustrates how grueling, challenging, and often unrewarding the life of migrant farmers could be. Just as George and Lennie dream of a better life on their own farm, the Great Plains farmers dreamed of finding a better life in California. The state's mild climate promised a longer growing season and, with soil favorable to a wider range of crops, it offered more opportunities to harvest. Despite these promises, though, very few found it to be the land of opportunity and plenty of which they dreamed.

PLOT OVERVIEW

WO MIGRANT WORKERS, George and Lennie, have been let off a bus miles away from the California farm where they are due to start work. George is a small, dark man with "sharp, strong features." Lennie, his companion, is his opposite, a giant of a man with a "shapeless" face. Overcome with thirst, the two stop in a clearing by a pool and decide to camp for the night. As the two converse, it becomes clear that Lennie has a mild mental disability, and is deeply devoted to George and dependent upon him for protection and guidance. George finds that Lennie, who loves petting soft things but often accidentally kills them, has been carrying and stroking a dead mouse. George angrily throws it away, fearing that Lennie might catch a disease from the dead animal. George complains loudly that his life would be easier without having to care for Lennie, but the reader senses that their friendship and devotion is mutual. He and Lennie share a dream of buying their own piece of land, farming it, and, much to Lennie's delight, keeping rabbits. George ends the night by treating Lennie to the story he often tells him about what life will be like in such an idyllic place.

The next day, the men report to the nearby ranch. George, fearing how the boss will react to Lennie, insists that he'll do all the talking. He lies, explaining that they travel together because they are cousins and that a horse kicked Lennie in the head when he was a child. They are hired. They meet Candy, an old "swamper," or handy-man, with a missing hand and an ancient dog, and Curley, the boss's mean-spirited son. Curley is newly married, possessive of his flirtatious wife, and full of jealous suspicion. Once George and Lennie are alone in the bunkhouse, Curley's wife appears and flirts with them. Lennie thinks she is "purty," but George, sensing the trouble that could come from tangling with this woman and her husband, warns Lennie to stay away from her. Soon, the ranch-hands return from the fields for lunch, and George and Lennie meet Slim, the skilled mule driver who wields great authority on the ranch. Slim comments on the rarity of friendship like that between George and Lennie. Carlson, another ranch-hand, suggests that since Slim's dog has just given birth, they should offer a puppy to Candy and shoot Candy's old, good-for-nothing dog.

The next day, George confides in Slim that he and Lennie are not cousins, but have been friends since childhood. He tells how Lennie has often gotten them into trouble. For instance, they were forced to flee their last job because Lennie tried to touch a woman's dress and was accused of rape. Slim agrees to give Lennie one of his puppies, and Carlson continues to badger Candy to kill his old dog. When Slim agrees with Carlson, saying that death would be a welcome relief to the suffering animal, Candy gives in. Carlson, before leading the dog outside, promises to do the job painlessly.

Slim goes to the barn to do some work, and Curley, who is maniacally searching for his wife, heads to the barn to accost Slim. Candy overhears George and Lennie discussing their plans to buy land, and offers his life's savings if they will let him live there too. The three make a pact to let no one else know of their plan. Slim returns to the bunkhouse, berating Curley for his suspicions. Curley, searching for an easy target for his anger, finds Lennie and picks a fight with him. Lennie crushes Curley's hand in the altercation. Slim warns Curley that if he tries to get George and Lennie fired, he will be the laughingstock of the farm.

The next night, most of the men go to the local brothel. Lennie is left with Crooks, the lonely, black stable-hand, and Candy. Curley's wife flirts with them, refusing to leave until the other men come home. She notices the cuts on Lennie's face and suspects that he, and not a piece of machinery as Curley claimed, is responsible for hurting her husband. This thought amuses her. The next day, Lennie accidentally kills his puppy in the barn. Curley's wife enters and consoles him. She admits that life with Curley is a disappointment, and wishes that she had followed her dream of becoming a movie star. Lennie tells her that he loves petting soft things, and she offers to let him feel her hair. When he grabs too tightly, she cries out. In his attempt to silence her, he accidentally breaks her neck.

Lennie flees back to a pool of the Salinas River that George had designated as a meeting place should either of them get into trouble. As the men back at the ranch discover what has happened and gather together a lynch party, George joins Lennie. Much to Lennie's surprise, George is not mad at him for doing "a bad thing." George begins to tell Lennie the story of the farm they will have together. As he describes the rabbits that Lennie will tend, the sound of the approaching lynch party grows louder. George shoots his friend in the back of the head.

When the other men arrive, George lets them believe that Lennie had the gun, and George wrestled it away from him and shot him. Only Slim understands what has really happened, that George has killed his friend out of mercy. Slim consolingly leads him away, and the other men, completely puzzled, watch them leave.

Character List

Lennie   A large, lumbering, childlike migrant worker. Due to his mild mental disability, Lennie completely depends upon George, his friend and traveling companion, for guidance and protection. The two men share a vision of a farm that they will own together, a vision that Lennie believes in wholeheartedly. Gentle and kind, Lennie nevertheless does not understand his own strength. His love of petting soft things, such as small animals, dresses, and people's hair, leads to disaster.

George   A small, wiry, quick-witted man who travels with, and cares for, Lennie. Although he frequently speaks of how much better his life would be without his caretaking responsibilities, George is obviously devoted to Lennie. George's behavior is motivated by the desire to protect Lennie and, eventually, deliver them both to the farm of their dreams. Though George is the source of the often-told story of life on their future farm, it is Lennie's childlike faith that enables George to actually believe his account of their future.

Candy   An aging ranch handyman, Candy lost his hand in an accident and worries about his future on the ranch. Fearing that his age is making him useless, he seizes on George's description of the farm he and Lennie will have, offering his life's savings if he can join George and Lennie in owning the land. The fate of Candy's ancient dog, which Carlson shoots in the back of the head in an alleged act of mercy, foreshadows the manner of Lennie's death.

Curley's wife The only female character in the novel, Curley's wife is never given a name and is only mentioned in reference to her husband. The men on the farm refer to her as a "tramp," a "tart," and a "looloo." Dressed in fancy, feathered red shoes, she represents the temptation of female sexuality in a male-dominated world.

9

Steinbeck depicts Curley's wife not as a villain, but rather as a victim. Like the ranch-hands, she is desperately lonely and has broken dreams of a better life.

Crooks Crooks, the black stable-hand, gets his name from his crooked back. Proud, bitter, and caustically funny, he is isolated from the other men because of the color of his skin. Despite himself, Crooks becomes fond of Lennie, and though he derisively claims to have seen countless men following empty dreams of buying their own land, he asks Lennie if he can go with them and hoe in the garden.

Curley The boss's son, Curley wears high-heeled boots to distinguish himself from the field hands. Rumored to be a champion prizefighter, he is a confrontational, mean-spirited, and aggressive young man who seeks to compensate for his small stature by picking fights with larger men. Recently married, Curley is plagued with jealous suspicions and is extremely possessive of his flirtatious young wife.

Slim A highly skilled mule driver and the acknowledged "prince" of the ranch, Slim is the only character who seems to be at peace with himself. The other characters often look to Slim for advice. For instance, only after Slim agrees that Candy should put his decrepit dog out of its misery does the old man agree to let Carlson shoot it. A quiet, insightful man, Slim alone understands the nature of the bond between George and Lennie, and comforts George at the novel's tragic ending.

Carlson A ranch-hand, Carlson complains bitterly about Candy's old, smelly dog. He convinces Candy to put the dog out of its misery. When Candy finally agrees, Carlson promises to execute the task without causing the animal any suffering. Later, George uses Carlson's gun to shoot Lennie.

The Boss   The stocky, well-dressed man in charge of the ranch, and Curley's father. He is never named and appears only once, but seems to be a fair-minded man. Candy happily reports that the boss once delivered a gallon of whiskey to the ranch-hands on Christmas Day.

Aunt Clara   Lennie's aunt, who cared for him until her death, does not actually appear in the novel except at the end, as a vision chastising Lennie for causing trouble for George. By all accounts, she was a kind, patient woman who took good care of Lennie and gave him plenty of mice to pet.

Whit   A ranch-hand.

CHARACTER LIST

ANALYSIS OF MAJOR CHARACTERS

LENNIE

Although Lennie is among the principal characters in *Of Mice and Men,* he is perhaps the least dynamic. He undergoes no significant changes, development, or growth throughout the novel and remains exactly as the reader encounters him in the opening pages. Simply put, he loves to pet soft things, is blindly devoted to George and their vision of the farm, and possesses incredible physical strength. Nearly every scene in which Lennie appears confirms these and only these characteristics.

Although Steinbeck's insistent repetition of these characteristics makes Lennie a rather flat character, Lennie's simplicity is central to Steinbeck's conception of the novel. *Of Mice and Men* is a very short work that manages to build up an extremely powerful impact. Since the tragedy depends upon the outcome seeming to be inevitable, the reader must know from the start that Lennie is doomed, and must be sympathetic to him. Steinbeck achieves these two feats by creating a protagonist who earns the reader's sympathy because of his utter helplessness in the face of the events that unfold. Lennie is totally defenseless. He cannot avoid the dangers presented by Curley, Curley's wife, or the world at large. His innocence raises him to a standard of pure goodness that is more poetic and literary than realistic. His enthusiasm for the vision of their future farm proves contagious as he convinces George, Candy, Crooks, and the reader that such a paradise might be possible. But he is a character whom Steinbeck sets up for disaster, a character whose innocence only seems to ensure his inevitable destruction.

GEORGE

Like Lennie, George can be defined by a few distinct characteristics. He is short-tempered but a loving and devoted friend, whose frequent protests against life with Lennie never weaken his commitment to protecting his friend. George's first words, a stern warning to Lennie not to drink so much lest he get sick, set the tone of their relationship. George may be terse and impatient at times, but he never strays from his primary purpose of protecting Lennie.

Unlike Lennie, however, George does change as the story progresses. The reader learns that he is capable of change and growth during his conversation with Slim, during which he admits that he once abused Lennie for his own amusement. From this incident George learned the moral lesson that it is wrong to take advantage of the weak. *Of Mice and Men* follows him toward a difficult realization that the world is designed to prey on the weak. At the start of the novel, George is something of an idealist. Despite his hardened, sometimes gruff exterior, he believes in the story of their future farm that he tells and retells to Lennie. He longs for the day when he can enjoy the freedom to leave work and see a baseball game. More important than a ball game, however, is the thought of living in safety and comfort with Lennie, free from people like Curley and Curley's wife, who seem to exist only to cause trouble for them. Lennie is largely responsible for George's belief in this safe haven, but eventually the predatory nature of the world asserts itself and George can no longer maintain that belief. By shooting Lennie, George spares his friend the merciless death that would be delivered by Curley's lynch mob, but he also puts to rest his own dream of a perfect, fraternal world.

CANDY

One of the book's major themes and several of its dominant symbols revolve around Candy. The old handyman, aging and left with only one hand as the result of an accident, worries that the boss will soon declare him useless and demand that he leave the ranch. Of course, life on the ranch—especially Candy's dog, once an impressive sheep herder but now toothless, foul-smelling, and brittle with age—supports Candy's fears. Past accomplishments and current emotional ties matter little, as Carson makes clear when he insists that Candy let him put the dog out of its misery. In such a world, Candy's dog serves as a harsh reminder of the fate that awaits anyone who outlives his usefulness.

For a brief time, however, the dream of living out his days with George and Lennie on their dream farm distracts Candy from this harsh reality. He deems the few acres of land they describe worthy of his hard-earned life's savings, which testifies to his desperate need to believe in a world kinder than the one in which he lives. Like George, Candy clings to the idea of having the freedom to take up or set aside work as he chooses. So strong is his devotion to this idea that, even after he discovers that Lennie has killed Curley's wife, he pleads for himself and George to go ahead and buy the farm as planned.

CURLEY'S WIFE

Of Mice and Men is not kind in its portrayal of women. In fact, women are treated with contempt throughout the course of the novel. Steinbeck generally depicts women as troublemakers who bring ruin on men and drive them mad. Curley's wife, who walks the ranch as a temptress, seems to be a prime example of this destructive tendency—Curley's already bad temper has only worsened since their wedding. Aside from wearisome wives, *Of Mice and Men* offers limited, rather misogynistic, descriptions of women who are either dead maternal figures or prostitutes.

Despite Steinbeck's rendering, Curley's wife emerges as a relatively complex and interesting character. Although her purpose is rather simple in the novel's opening pages—she is the "tramp," "tart," and "bitch" that threatens to destroy male happiness and longevity—her appearances later in the novel become more complex. When she confronts Lennie, Candy, and Crooks in the stable, she admits to feeling a kind of shameless dissatisfaction with her life. Her vulnerability at this moment and later—when she admits to Lennie her dream of becoming a movie star—makes her utterly human and much more interesting than the stereotypical vixen in fancy red shoes. However, it also reinforces the novel's grim worldview. In her moment of greatest vulnerability, Curley's wife seeks out even greater weaknesses in others, preying upon Lennie's mental handicap, Candy's debilitating age, and the color of Crooks's skin in order to steel herself against harm.

CROOKS

Crooks is a lively, sharp-witted, black stable-hand, who takes his name from his crooked back. Like most of the characters in the novel, he admits that he is extremely lonely. When Lennie visits him in his room, his reaction reveals this fact. At first, he turns Lennie away, hoping to prove a point that if he, as a black man, is not allowed in white men's houses, then whites are not allowed in

his, but his desire for company ultimately wins out and he invites Lennie to sit with him. Like Curley's wife, Crooks is a disempowered character who turns his vulnerability into a weapon to attack those who are even weaker. He plays a cruel game with Lennie, suggesting to him that George is gone for good. Only when Lennie threatens him with physical violence does he relent. Crooks exhibits the corrosive effects that loneliness can have on a person; his character evokes sympathy as the origins of his cruel behavior are made evident. Perhaps what Crooks wants more than anything else is a sense of belonging—to enjoy simple pleasures such as the right to enter the bunkhouse or to play cards with the other men. This desire would explain why, even though he has reason to doubt George and Lennie's talk about the farm that they want to own, Crooks cannot help but ask if there might be room for him to come along and hoe in the garden.

THEMES, MOTIFS & SYMBOLS

THEMES

Themes are the fundamental and often universal ideas explored in a literary work.

THE PREDATORY NATURE OF HUMAN EXISTENCE

Of Mice and Men teaches a grim lesson about the nature of human existence. Nearly all of the characters, including George, Lennie, Candy, Crooks, and Curley's wife, admit, at one time or another, to having a profound sense of loneliness and isolation. Each desires the comfort of a friend, but will settle for the attentive ear of a stranger. Curley's wife admits to Candy, Crooks, and Lennie that she is unhappily married, and Crooks tells Lennie that life is no good without a companion to turn to in times of confusion and need. The characters are rendered helpless by their isolation, and yet, even at their weakest, they seek to destroy those who are even weaker than they. Perhaps the most powerful example of this cruel tendency is when Crooks criticizes Lennie's dream of the farm and his dependence on George. Having just admitted his own vulnerabilities—he is a black man with a crooked back who longs for companionship—Crooks zeroes in on Lennie's own weaknesses.

In scenes such as this one, Steinbeck records a profound human truth: oppression does not come only from the hands of the strong or the powerful. Crooks seems at his strongest when he has nearly reduced Lennie to tears for fear that something bad has happened to George, just as Curley's wife feels most powerful when she threatens to have Crooks lynched. The novel suggests that the most visible kind of strength—that used to oppress others—is itself born of weakness.

FRATERNITY AND THE IDEALIZED MALE FRIENDSHIP

One of the reasons that the tragic end of George and Lennie's friendship has such a profound impact is that one senses that the friends have, by the end of the novel, lost a dream larger than themselves. The farm on which George and Lennie plan to live—a place that

17

no one ever reaches—has a magnetic quality, as Crooks points out. After hearing a description of only a few sentences, Candy is completely drawn in by its magic. Crooks has witnessed countless men fall under the same silly spell, and still he cannot help but ask Lennie if he can have a patch of garden to hoe there. The men in *Of Mice and Men* desire to come together in a way that would allow them to be like brothers to one another. That is, they want to live with one another's best interests in mind, to protect each other, and to know that there is someone in the world dedicated to protecting them. Given the harsh, lonely conditions under which these men live, it should come as no surprise that they idealize friendships between men in such a way.

Ultimately, however, the world is too harsh and predatory a place to sustain such relationships. Lennie and George, who come closest to achieving this ideal of brotherhood, are forced to separate tragically. With this, a rare friendship vanishes, but the rest of the world—represented by Curley and Carlson, who watch George stumble away with grief from his friend's dead body—fails to acknowledge or appreciate it.

THEMES

The Impossibility of the American Dream

Most of the characters in *Of Mice and Men* admit, at one point or another, to dreaming of a different life. Before her death, Curley's wife confesses her desire to be a movie star. Crooks, bitter as he is, allows himself the pleasant fantasy of hoeing a patch of garden on Lennie's farm one day, and Candy latches on desperately to George's vision of owning a couple of acres. Before the action of the novel begins, circumstances have robbed most of the characters of these wishes. Curley's wife, for instance, has resigned herself to an unfulfilling marriage. What makes all of these dreams typically American is that the dreamers wish for untarnished happiness, for the freedom to follow their own desires. George and Lennie's dream of owning a farm, which would enable them to sustain themselves, and, most important, offer them protection from an inhospitable world, represents a prototypically American ideal. Their journey, which awakens George to the impossibility of this dream, sadly proves that the bitter Crooks is right: such paradises of freedom, contentment, and safety are not to be found in this world.

MOTIFS

Motifs are recurring structures, contrasts, and literary devices that can help to develop and inform the text's major themes.

THE CORRUPTING POWER OF WOMEN

The portrayal of women in *Of Mice and Men* is limited and unflattering. We learn early on that Lennie and George are on the run from the previous ranch where they worked, due to encountering trouble there with a woman. Misunderstanding Lennie's love of soft things, a woman accused him of rape for touching her dress. George berates Lennie for his behavior, but is convinced that women are always the cause of such trouble. Their enticing sexuality, he believes, tempts men to behave in ways they would otherwise not.

A visit to the "flophouse" (a cheap hotel, or brothel) is enough of women for George, and he has no desire for a female companion or wife. Curley's wife, the only woman to appear in *Of Mice and Men,* seems initially to support George's view of marriage. Dissatisfied with her marriage to a brutish man and bored with life on the ranch, she is constantly looking for excitement or trouble. In one of her more revealing moments, she threatens to have the black stable-hand lynched if he complains about her to the boss. Her insistence on flirting with Lennie seals her unfortunate fate. Although Steinbeck does, finally, offer a sympathetic view of Curley's wife by allowing her to voice her unhappiness and her own dream for a better life, women have no place in the author's idealized vision of a world structured around the brotherly bonds of men.

LONELINESS AND COMPANIONSHIP

Many of the characters admit to suffering from profound loneliness. George sets the tone for these confessions early in the novel when he reminds Lennie that the life of a ranch-hand is among the loneliest of lives. Men like George who migrate from farm to farm rarely have anyone to look to for companionship and protection. As the story develops, Candy, Crooks, and Curley's wife all confess their deep loneliness. The fact that they admit to complete strangers their fear of being cast off shows their desperation. In a world without friends to confide in, strangers will have to do. Each of these characters searches for a friend, someone to help them measure the world, as Crooks says. In the end, however, companionship of his kind seems unattainable. For George, the hope of such companionship dies with Lennie, and true to his original estimation, he will go through life alone.

STRENGTH AND WEAKNESS

Steinbeck explores different types of strength and weakness throughout the novel. The first, and most obvious, is physical strength. As the novel opens, Steinbeck shows how Lennie possesses physical strength beyond his control, as when he cannot help killing the mice. Great physical strength is, like money, quite valuable to men in George and Lennie's circumstances. Curley, as a symbol of authority on the ranch and a champion boxer, makes this clear immediately by using his brutish strength and violent temper to intimidate the men and his wife.

Physical strength is not the only force that oppresses the men in the novel. It is the rigid, predatory human tendencies, not Curley, that defeat Lennie and George in the end. Lennie's physical size and strength prove powerless; in the face of these universal laws, he is utterly defenseless and therefore disposable.

SYMBOLS

Symbols are objects, characters, figures, and colors used to represent abstract ideas or concepts.

GEORGE AND LENNIE'S FARM

The farm that George constantly describes to Lennie—those few acres of land on which they will grow their own food and tend their own livestock—is one of the most powerful symbols in the book. It seduces not only the other characters but also the reader, who, like the men, wants to believe in the possibility of the free, idyllic life it promises. Candy is immediately drawn in by the dream, and even the cynical Crooks hopes that Lennie and George will let him live there too. A paradise for men who want to be masters of their own lives, the farm represents the possibility of freedom, self-reliance, and protection from the cruelties of the world.

LENNIE'S PUPPY

Lennie's puppy is one of several symbols that represent the victory of the strong over the weak. Lennie kills the puppy accidentally, as he has killed many mice before, by virtue of his failure to recognize his own strength. Although no other character can match Lennie's physical strength, the huge Lennie will soon meet a fate similar to that of his small puppy. Like an innocent animal, Lennie is unaware of the vicious, predatory powers that surround him.

CANDY'S DOG

In the world *Of Mice and Men* describes, Candy's dog represents the fate awaiting anyone who has outlived his or her purpose. Once a fine sheepdog, useful on the ranch, Candy's mutt is now debilitated by age. Candy's sentimental attachment to the animal—his plea that Carlson let the dog live for no other reason than that Candy raised it from a puppy—means nothing at all on the ranch. Although Carlson promises to kill the dog painlessly, his insistence that the old animal must die supports a cruel natural law that the strong will dispose of the weak. Candy internalizes this lesson, for he fears that he himself is nearing an age when he will no longer be useful at the ranch, and therefore no longer welcome.

SYMBOLS

Summary & Analysis

Section 1

From the opening of the novel to George instructing Lennie in preparation for their arrival at the ranch (nightfall)

Summary

The novel opens with the description of a riverbed in rural California, a beautiful, wooded area at the base of "golden foothill slopes." A path runs to the river, used by boys going swimming and riffraff coming down from the highway. Two men walk along the path. The first, George, is small, wiry, and sharp-featured, while his companion, Lennie, is large and awkward. They are both dressed in denim, farmhand attire.

As they reach a clearing, Lennie stops to drink from the river, and George warns him not to drink too much or he will get sick, as he did the night before. As their conversation continues, it becomes clear that the larger man has a mild mental disability, and that his companion looks out for his safety. George begins to complain about the bus driver who dropped them off a long way from their intended destination—a ranch on which they are due to begin work. Lennie interrupts him to ask where they are going. His companion impatiently reminds him of their movements over the past few days, and then notices that Lennie is holding a dead mouse. George takes it away from him. Lennie insists that he is not responsible for killing the mouse, that he just wanted to pet it, but George loses his temper and throws it across the stream. George warns Lennie that they are going to work on a ranch, and that he must behave himself when they meet the boss. George does not want any trouble of the kind they encountered in Weed, the last place they worked.

George decides that they will stay in the clearing for the night, and as they prepare their bean supper, Lennie crosses the stream and recovers the mouse, only to have George find him out immediately and take the mouse away again. Apparently, Lennie's Aunt Clara used to give him mice to pet, but he tends to "break" small creatures unintentionally when he shows his affection for them, killing them because he doesn't know his own strength. As the two men sit down to eat, Lennie asks for ketchup. This request launches George into a long speech about Lennie's ungratefulness. George complains that he could get along much better if he didn't have to care for Lennie. He uses the incident that got them chased out of Weed as a case in point. Lennie, a lover of soft things, stroked the fabric of a girl's dress, and would not let go. The locals assumed he assaulted her, and ran them out of town.

> *With us it ain't like that. We got a future. We got somebody to talk to that gives a damn about us.*
>
> *(See* QUOTATIONS, *p. 41)*

After this tirade, George feels sorry for losing his temper and apologizes by telling Lennie's favorite story, the plan for their future happiness. The life of a ranch-hand, according to George, is one of the loneliest in the world, and most men working on ranches have no one to look out for them. But he and Lennie have each other, and someday, as soon as they manage to save enough money, they will buy a farm together and, as Lennie puts it, "live off the fatta the lan'." They will grow their own food, raise livestock, and keep rabbits, which Lennie will tend. This familiar story cheers both of them up. As night falls, George tells Lennie that if he encounters any trouble while working at the ranch, he is to return to this clearing, hide in the bushes, and wait for George to come.

SUMMARY & ANALYSIS

ANALYSIS

The clearing into which Lennie and George wander evokes Eden in its serenity and beauty. Steinbeck wisely opens the novel with this idyllic scene, for it creates a background for the idealized friendship between the men and introduces the romanticized dream of farm life that they share. The opening pages establish a sense of purity and perfection that the world, which will prove to be cruel and predatory, cannot sustain. Steinbeck also solidly establishes the relationship between George and Lennie within the first few pages of dialogue. Their speech is that of uneducated laborers, but is emotionally rich and often lyrical.

Because George and Lennie are not particularly dynamic characters (neither of them changes significantly during the course of the narrative), the impression the reader gets from these early pages persists throughout the novel. Lennie's and George's behavior is relatively static. Lennie's sweet innocence, the undying devotion he shows George, and his habit of petting soft things are his major defining traits from the opening pages to the final scene.

Just as constant are George's blustery rants about how much easier life would be without the burden of caring for Lennie, and unconvincing speeches that always end by revealing his love for and desire to protect his friend.

Some critics of the novel consider George, and especially Lennie, somewhat flat representations of purity, goodness, and fraternal devotion, rather than convincing portraits of complex, conflicted human beings. They charge Steinbeck with being excessively sentimental in his portrayal of his protagonists, his romanticization of male friendship, and in the deterministic plot that seems designed to destroy this friendship. Others, however, contend that any exaggeration in *Of Mice and Men,* like in so many of Steinbeck's other works, is meant to comment on the plight of the downtrodden, to make the reader sympathize with people who society and storytellers often deem unworthy because of their class, physical or mental capabilities, or the color of their skin.

Whether or not these issues constitute a flaw in the novel, it is true that Steinbeck places George, Lennie, and their relationship on a rather high pedestal. Nowhere is this more clear than in the story George constantly tells about the farm they one day plan to own. This piece of land represents a world in which the two men can live together just as they are, without dangers and without apologies. No longer will they be run out of towns like Weed or be subject to the demeaning and backbreaking will of others. As the novel progresses and their situation worsens, George and Lennie's desire to attain the farm they dream about grows more desperate. Their vision becomes so powerful that it will eventually attract other men, who will beg to be a part of it. George's story of the farm, as well as George and Lennie's mutual devotion, lays the groundwork for one of the novel's dominant themes: the idealized sense of friendship among men.

True to the nature of tragedy, Steinbeck makes the vision of the farm so beautiful and the fraternal bond between George and Lennie so strong in order to place his protagonists at a considerable height from which to fall. From the very beginning, Steinbeck heavily foreshadows the doom that awaits the men. The clearing into which the two travelers stumble may resemble Eden, but it is, in fact, a world with dangers lurking at every turn. The rabbits that sit like "gray, sculptured stones" hurry for cover at the sound of footsteps, hinting at the predatory world that will finally destroy Lennie and George's dream. The dead mouse in Lennie's pocket serves as a potent symbol of the end that awaits weak, unsuspecting creatures. After all, despite Lennie's great physical size and strength, his childlike mental capabilities render him as helpless as a mouse.

Steinbeck's repeated comparisons between Lennie and animals (bears, horses, terriers) reinforce the impending sense of doom. Animals in the novel, from field mice to Candy's dog to Lennie's puppy, all die untimely deaths. The novel's tragic course of action seems even more inevitable when one considers Lennie's troublesome behavior that got George and Lennie chased out of Weed, and George's anticipatory insistence that they designate a meeting place should any problems arise.

SECTION 2

From Lennie and George's arrival at the ranch to an unpleasant encounter with Curley

SUMMARY

The next day, Lennie and George make their way to the ranch bunkhouse, where they are greeted by Candy, an aging "swamper," or handyman, who has lost his right hand. The bunkhouse is an unadorned building where the men sleep on "burlap ticking" and keep their few possessions in apple boxes that have been nailed to the walls. George is dismayed to find a can of lice powder in his bunk, but Candy assures him that he's in no danger of being infested, since the man who slept there before George was remarkably clean. George asks about the boss, and Candy reports that although the boss was angry that George and Lennie did not arrive the previous night as he had expected them to, he can be a "pretty nice fella." Candy relates how the boss gave the men a gallon of whiskey for Christmas, which immediately impresses George.

The boss appears and questions the pair about their late arrival. George blames it on the bus driver, who, he claims, lied to them about their proximity to the ranch. When the boss asks about their skills and previous employment, George speaks for Lennie to prevent him from revealing his lack of intelligence. When Lennie momentarily forgets George's instructions and speaks, George becomes visibly nervous. Their behavior strikes the boss as suspicious, and he asks why George feels the need to take such good care of his companion. He wonders if George is taking advantage of a man who lacks the faculties to take care of himself. George replies that Lennie is his cousin and was kicked in the head by a horse when he was young, so George has to look out for him. The boss remains suspicious and warns George not to try to pull anything over on him. Nonetheless, they are assigned to one of the grain teams, working under a man named Slim.

Once the boss leaves the bunkhouse, George berates Lennie for having spoken up. Candy overhears George telling Lennie that he is glad they are not actually related. George warns Candy that he doesn't appreciate other people sticking their noses in his business, but Candy assures him that he minds his own business and has no interest in their affairs. Accompanying Candy is an ancient, half-blind sheepdog, an animal that the old man has raised since it was a puppy. Soon enough, Curley, the boss's son, a small young man who wears a Vaseline-filled work glove on his left hand and high-heeled boots to distinguish himself from the laborers, joins them. Curley, an aggressive and malicious ex-boxer, immediately senses that he might have some fun at Lennie's expense, and begins to demand that "the big guy talk." After Curley leaves, Candy explains that Curley loves beating up big guys, "kind of like he's mad at 'em because he ain't a big guy." Curley's temper has only gotten worse since his recent marriage to a "tart" who enjoys flirting with the ranch-hands.

Candy leaves to prepare wash basins for the men who will soon return from the fields, and George tells Lennie to steer clear of Curley, because fighting the "bastard" will likely cost them their jobs. Lennie agrees, assuring George that he doesn't want any trouble. George reminds him again of the meeting place they agreed on should anything go wrong. At that moment, Curley's wife, a pretty, heavily made-up woman with a nasal voice, appears. She claims to be looking for her husband and flirts with the two men and Slim, the skilled mule driver, who passes by outside. Slim tells her that Curley has gone into the house, and she hurries off. Lennie speaks admiringly of how "purty" the woman is, and George angrily orders him to stay away from "that bitch." Lennie, suddenly frightened, complains that he wants to leave the ranch, but George reminds him that they need to make some money before they can buy their own land and live their dream.

Slim enters the bunkhouse. His talents make him one of the most important and respected men on the ranch. There is a "gravity in his manner," and everyone stops talking and listens when he speaks. He converses with Lennie and George, and is quietly impressed by their friendship, appreciating the fact that they look out for one another. The men are joined by Carlson, another ranch-hand. Carlson asks about Slim's dog, which has just given birth to nine puppies. Slim reports that he drowned four of the puppies immediately because their mother would have been unable to feed them. Carlson suggests that they convince Candy to shoot his old, worthless mutt and raise one of the pups instead. The triangle rings for dinner, and the men filter out of the bunkhouse, with Lennie suddenly excited by the prospect of having a puppy. As George and Lennie prepare to leave, Curley appears again, looking for his wife, and hurries off angrily when they tell him where she went. George expresses his dislike for Curley, and comments that he is afraid he will "tangle" with Curley himself.

ANALYSIS

Once George and Lennie arrive at the bunkhouse, the difficulties of the lives they lead become starkly apparent. There are few comforts in their quarters; the men sleep on rough burlap mattresses and do not own anything that cannot fit into an apple box. George's fear that lice and roaches infest his bunk furthers the image of the struggles of such a life. This section also immediately and painfully establishes the cruel, predatory nature of the world. Carlson's belief that Candy should replace his old dog with a healthy newborn puppy signals a world in which the lives of the weak and debilitated are considered unworthy of protection or preservation. The ranch-hands' world has limited resources, and only the strongest will survive. As Slim, who voluntarily drowns four of his dog's nine puppies, makes clear, there is little room or tolerance for the weak, especially when resources are limited. Throughout the course of the novel, nearly all of the characters will confront this grim reality. Not only does the ranch represent a society that does not consider the welfare of its weaker members, but it also stands as one in which those who hold power wield it irresponsibly.

Though the boss seems fair-minded, treating his men to whiskey at Christmas and giving Lennie and George the benefit of the doubt, he is an unimportant character. Instead, his son Curley embodies authority on the ranch. In the novel's vision of the world, Curley represents the vicious and belligerent way in which social power tends to manifest itself. Given Curley's temperament, he serves as a natural foil—a character whose emotions or actions contrast with those of other characters—for both the gentle Lennie and the self-assured Slim. Whereas Curley is plagued by self-doubts that cause him to explode violently, Slim possesses a quiet competence that earns him the respect of everyone on the ranch. Like Curley, Slim stands as an authority figure. The men on the ranch look to him for advice, and, later, even Curley will deliver an uncharacteristic apology after wrongly accusing Slim of fooling around with his wife. Slim's authority comes from his self-possession; he needs neither the approval nor the failure of others to confirm his stature. Curley's strength, on the other hand, depends upon his ability to dominate and defeat those weaker than him.

George and Lennie immediately feel the threat that Curley's presence poses. To avoid getting into trouble with Curley, they promise to stick even closer to each other than usual. Their friendship is rare and impressive. Slim, who wonders why more men don't travel around together and theorizes that maybe it's because everyone is scared of everyone else, appreciates the closeness of their friendship. In the novel as a whole, Steinbeck celebrates and romanticizes the bonds between men. The men in *Of Mice and Men* dominate the ranch and long, more than anything else, to live peaceful, untroubled lives in the company of other men. The only female character who has an active role in the book is Curley's wife, who, significantly, Steinbeck never names, and identifies only in reference to her husband. Other female characters are mentioned in passing, but with the exception of the maternal Aunt Clara, who cared for Lennie before her death, they are invariably prostitutes or troublemakers.

Even with all of its concern for treating with dignity the lives of the socially disempowered, *Of Mice and Men* derogatorily assigns women only two lowly functions: caretakers of men, and sex objects. Regardless of their place in the real world, the novel altogether dismisses women from its vision of paradise. Female sexuality is described as a trap laid to ensnare and ruin men. George and Lennie imagine themselves alone, without wives or women to complicate their vision of tending the land and raising rabbits. Much like a traditional, conservative Christian interpretation of the myth of man's expulsion from the Garden of Eden, the novel presents women as a temptation leading to man's fall from perfection.

SECTION 3

From Slim and George returning to the bunkhouse to George comforting Lennie after the fight with Curley

SUMMARY

At the end of the workday, Slim and George return to the bunk-house. Slim has agreed to give one of the pups to Lennie, and George thanks him for his kindness, insisting that Lennie is "dumb as hell," but is neither crazy nor mean. Slim appreciates George's friendship with Lennie, saying that it is a welcome change in a world where no one ever "seems to give a damn about nobody." George confides in Slim the story of how he and Lennie came to be companions. They were born in the same town, and George took charge of Lennie after the death of Lennie's Aunt Clara. At first, George admits, he pushed Lennie around, getting him to do ridiculous things, such as jumping into a river even though he didn't know how to swim. After watching his friend nearly drown, George felt ashamed of his behavior. Since that day, he has taken good care of his companion, protecting him even when he gets in trouble. For example, in Weed, the last town where they worked, Lennie wanted to touch the fabric of a girl's red dress. When she pulled away, Lennie became frightened and held on to her until George hit him over the head to make him let go. The girl accused Lennie of rape, and George and Lennie had to hide in an irrigation ditch to escape a lynch mob.

Lennie comes into the bunkhouse, carrying his new puppy under his coat. George berates him for taking the little creature away from its mother. As Lennie returns the puppy to the litter, Candy and Carlson appear. Carlson begins to complain again about Candy's dog, saying that it stinks and that it "ain't no good to himself." He urges Candy to shoot the animal. Candy replies that he has had the dog for too many years to kill it, but Carlson continues to pressure him. Eventually Slim joins in, suggesting that Candy would be put-ting a suffering animal out if its misery. Slim offers him a puppy and urges him to let Carlson shoot the dog. Another farmhand, Whit, enters and shows Slim a letter written by a man they used to work with published in a pulp magazine. The short letter praises the magazine. As the men marvel over it, Carlson offers to kill the dog quickly by shooting it in the back of the head. Reluctantly, Candy gives in. Carlson takes the dog outside, promising Slim that he will bury the corpse. After a few awkward moments of silence, the men hear a shot ring out, and Candy turns his face to the wall.

Crooks, the black stable-hand, comes in and tells Slim that he has warmed some tar to put on a mule's foot. After Slim leaves, the other men play cards and discuss Curley's wife, agreeing that she will make trouble for someone; as George says, "She's a jailbait all set on the trigger." Whit invites George to accompany them to a local whorehouse the following night. Whit discusses the merits of old Susy's place over Clara's, it being cheaper and having nice chairs, but George comments that he cannot afford to waste his money because he and Lennie are trying to put together a "stake." Lennie and Carlson come in. Carlson cleans his gun and avoids looking at Candy. Curley appears looking for his wife again. Full of jealousy and suspicion, he asks where Slim is. When he learns that Slim is in the barn, he storms off in that direction, followed by Whit and Carlson, who hope to see a fight.

George asks Lennie if he saw Slim with Curley's wife in the barn, and Lennie says no. George warns his companion against the trouble that women cause, and then Lennie asks him to describe the farm that they hope to buy. As George talks, Candy listens and becomes excited by the idea of such a beautiful place. He asks if the place really exists. George is guarded at first, but soon says that it does and that the owners are desperate to sell it. Overcome with hope, Candy offers to contribute his life's savings if they allow him to live there too. Since he is old and crippled, he worries that the ranch will let him go soon. The men agree that after a month of work at this ranch, they will have enough money saved to make a down payment on the house. George tells the other two not to tell anyone else about their plan. As they hear the other men's voices approaching, Candy says quietly to George that he should have shot his old dog himself, and not let a stranger do it.

Slim, Curley, Carlson, and Whit return. Curley apologizes to Slim for his suspicions, and then the other men mock him. Knowing that Slim is too strong to be beaten in a fight, Curley looks to vent his rage elsewhere. He finds an easy target in Lennie, who is still dreaming of the farm and smiling with childlike delight. Though Lennie begs to be left alone, Curley attacks him. He throws several punches, bloodying Lennie's face, and hits him in the gut before George urges Lennie to fight back. On George's command, Lennie grabs Curley's right hand and breaks it effortlessly. As Slim leads Curley away to a doctor, he warns him not to have George and Lennie fired, or he will be made the laughingstock of the ranch. Curley consents not to attempt to have them fired. George comforts Lennie, telling him that the fight was not his fault and that he has nothing to fear. Lennie's only fear is that he will not be allowed to tend the rabbits on their farm. George assures him that he will.

ANALYSIS

During George's conversation with Slim, Steinbeck establishes the origins of Lennie and George's relationship in a few broad strokes. Theirs is a childhood relationship grown into a rare adult companionship. After years of torturing and taking advantage of his friend, George had a moral awakening, realizing that it is wrong to make a weaker living being suffer for sport. This conviction runs counter to the cruel nature of the world of the ranch-hands, in which the strong hunt down and do away with the weak. In this section, the death of Candy's dog testifies to the pitiless process by which the strong attack and eliminate the weak. Candy's dog, although no longer useful at corralling sheep, is of great importance to the old swamper. Candy's emotional attachment to the dog is clear. Regardless, allowing the animal to live out its days is not an option in this cruel environment. Carlson insists that the animal's infirmity makes it unworthy of such devotion. The most comfort he can offer is to assure Candy that he will kill the dog mercifully and quickly. When Slim, the novel's most trusted source of wisdom, agrees, he only confirms that their world is one that offers the weak and disempowered little hope of protection.

> "We'd just go to her," George said. "We wouldn't ask nobody if we could. Jus' say, 'We'll go to her,' an' we would. Jus' milk the cow and sling some grain to the chickens an' go to her."
>
> (See QUOTATIONS, p. 42)

Nearly all of the characters in *Of Mice and Men* are disempowered in some way. Whether because of a physical or mental handicap, age, class, race, or gender, almost everyone finds him- or herself outside the structures of social power, and each suffers greatly as a result. Inflexible rules dictate that old men are sent away from the ranch when they are no longer useful and black workers are refused entrance to the bunkhouse. While the world described in the novel offers no protection for the suffering, there are small comforts. Lennie and George's story is one such reprieve. The power of their vision of a simple life on an idyllic little farm rests in its ability to soothe the afflicted. In the opening chapter, this vision acts like a salve for Lennie and George after their tumultuous departure from Weed; now, it rouses Candy out of mourning for his dog. As soon as the lonely old man overhears George and Lennie discussing their plans, he seems pitifully eager to join in this paradise. Talking about it again also manages to calm and comfort Lennie after his upsetting run-in with Curley. Despite the fact that with Candy's help the possibility of purchasing the farm grows more real for George and Lennie than ever before, it is clear that tragic events will intervene. George's story will prove to be only a temporary escape from the world's troubles, not a cure.

Steinbeck advances the narrative toward the inevitable tragedy through many instances of foreshadowing in this section. The story of Lennie's behavior in Weed and his performance in the fight with Curley establish his tendency to exert great strength when confused and frightened. Combined with George's earlier observation that Lennie kept accidentally killing mice while petting them, these events heavily anticipate Lennie's deadly interaction with Curley's wife in the novel's climactic scene. Furthermore, the method by which Carlson kills Candy's dog—with a painless shot to the back of the head—sadly mirrors the way George will choose to murder his dearest friend. It is no coincidence that soon after George confides in Slim that he has known Lennie since childhood, Candy pathetically says that he could never kill his dog, since he has "had him since he was a pup." Most significant is Candy's quiet comment to George that he wishes he had shot his old dog himself and not allowed a stranger to do it, a distinct foreshadowing of the decision George will make to kill Lennie himself rather than let him be killed by Curley and the others.

Section 4

From Lennie talking to Crooks in the harness room to after Curley's wife threatening Crooks

Summary

The next evening, Saturday, Crooks sits on his bunk in the harness room. The black stable-hand has a crooked back—the source of his nickname—and is described as a "proud, aloof man" who spends much of his time reading. Lennie, who has been in the barn tending to his puppy, appears in the doorway, looking for company. Crooks tells him to go away, saying that if he, as a black man, is not allowed in the white quarters, then white men are not allowed in *his*. Lennie does not understand. He innocently reports that everyone else has gone into town and that he saw Crooks's light on and thought he could come in and keep him company. Finally, despite himself, Crooks yields to Lennie's "disarming smile" and invites him in.

> *Just like heaven. Ever'body wants a little piece of lan'.*
> *I read plenty of books out here. Nobody never gets to*
> *heaven, and nobody gets no land.*
>
> (See QUOTATIONS, p. 44)

Soon enough, Lennie forgets his promise to keep the farm a secret and begins to babble cheerfully about the place that he and George will buy someday. Crooks does not believe him, assuming that the fantasy is part of Lennie's mental disability. He tells Lennie about his own life, recounting his early days on a chicken farm when white children visited and played with him. Still, he says, he felt keenly alone even then. His family was the only black family for miles, and his father constantly warned him against keeping company with their white neighbors. The importance of this instruction escaped Crooks as a child, but he says that he has come to understand it perfectly. Now, as the only black man on the ranch, he resents the unfair social norms that require him to sleep alone in the stable. Feeling weak and vulnerable himself, Crooks cruelly suggests that George might never return from town. He enjoys torturing Lennie, until Lennie becomes angry and threatens Crooks, demanding to know "Who hurt George?" Crooks hastily backs down, promising that George will come back, and begins to talk about his childhood again, which returns Lennie to his dreams of owning the farm. Crooks bitterly says that every ranch-hand has the same dream. He adds that he has seen countless men go on about the same piece of land, but nothing ever comes of it. A little piece of land, Crooks claims, is as hard to find as heaven.

Candy eventually joins them, entering Crooks's room for the first time in all of the years they have worked together. Both men are uncomfortable at first but Candy is respectful and Crooks pleased to have more company. Candy talks to Lennie about raising rabbits on the farm. He has been busy calculating numbers and thinks he knows how the farm can make some money with rabbits. Crooks continues to belittle their dream until Candy insists that they already have the land picked out and nearly all the money they'll need to buy it. This news piques the black man's interest. Shyly, Crooks suggests that maybe they could take him along with them. But Curley's wife appears and interrupts the men's daydreaming.

Curley's wife asks about her husband, then says she knows that the men went to a brothel, cruelly observing that "they left all the weak ones here." Crooks and Candy tell her to go away, but instead she starts talking about her loneliness and her unhappy marriage. Candy insists that she leave and says proudly that even if she got them fired, they could go off and buy their own place to live. Curley's wife laughs at him, then bitterly complains about her life with Curley. She sums up her situation, admitting that she feels pathetic to want company so desperately that she is willing to talk to the likes of Crooks, Candy, and Lennie. She asks what happened to her husband's hand, and does not believe the men when they insist that he got it caught in a machine. She teases Lennie about the bruises on his face, deducing that he got injured in the scuffle with Curley.

Fed up, Crooks insists that she leave before he tells the boss about her wicked ways, and she responds by asking if he knows what she can do to him if he says anything. The implication is clear that she could easily have him lynched, and he cowers. Candy says that he hears the men coming back, which finally makes her leave, but not before she tells Lennie that she is glad he beat her husband. George appears, and criticizes Candy for talking about their farm in front of other people. As the white men leave Crooks, he changes his mind about going to the farm with them, calling out, "I wouldn' want to go no place like that."

Analysis

This section introduces the character of Crooks, who has previously only made a brief appearance. Like the other men in the novel, Crooks is a lonely figure. Like Candy, a physical disability sets him apart from the other workers, and makes him worry that he will soon wear out his usefulness on the ranch. Crooks's isolation is compounded by the fact that, as a black man, he is relegated to sleep in a room in the stables; he is not allowed in the white ranch-hands' quarters and not invited to play cards or visit brothels with them. He feels this isolation keenly and has an understandably bitter reaction to it.

The character of Crooks is an authorial achievement on several levels. First, Crooks broadens the social significance of the novel by offering race as another context by which to understand Steinbeck's central thesis. The reader has already witnessed how the world conspires to crush men who are debilitated by physical or mental infirmities. With Crooks, the same unjust, predatory rules hold true for people based on the color of their skin. Crooks's race is the only weapon Curley's wife needs to render him completely powerless. When she suggests that she could have him lynched, he can mount no defense. The second point to note about Crooks's character is that he is less of an easily categorized type than the characters that surround him. Lennie might be a bit too innocent and Curley a bit too antagonistic for the reader to believe in them as real, complex human beings.

Crooks, on the other hand, exhibits an ambivalence that makes him one of the more complicated and believably human characters in the novel. He is able to condemn Lennie's talk of the farm as foolishness, but becomes seduced by it nonetheless. Furthermore, bitter as he is about his exclusion from the other men, Crooks feels grateful for Lennie's company. When Candy, too, enters Crooks's room, it is "difficult for Crooks to conceal his pleasure with anger." Yet, as much as he craves companionship, he cannot help himself from lashing out at Lennie with unkind suggestions that George has been hurt and will not return.

Crooks's behavior serves to further the reader's understanding of the predatory nature of the ranch-hands' world. Not only will the strong attack the weak but the weak will attack the weaker. In a better world, Crooks, Lennie, and even Curley's wife might have formed an alliance, wherein the various attributes for which society punishes them—being black, being mentally disabled, and being female, respectively—would bring them together. On the ranch, however, they are pitted against one another. Crooks berates Lennie until Lennie threatens to do him physical harm; Crooks accuses Curley's wife of being a tramp; and she, in turn, threatens to have him lynched. As she stands in the doorway to Crooks's room looking over at the men, she draws attention to their weaknesses. Deriding them as "a nigger an' a dum-dum and a lousy ol' sheep," she viciously but accurately lays bare the perceptions by which they are ostracized by society. Like Crooks, Curley's wife displays a heartbreaking vulnerability in this scene, readily and shamelessly confessing her loneliness and her unhappy marriage. But because she is as pathetic as the men who sit before her, she seeks out the sources of their weakness and attacks them.

SECTION 5

*From Lennie stroking his dead puppy in the barn to Curley
leading a mob of men to find and kill Lennie*

SUMMARY

It is Sunday afternoon and Lennie is alone in the barn, sitting in the
hay and stroking the dead body of his puppy. He talks to himself,
asking the animal why it died: "You ain't so little as mice. I didn't
bounce you hard." Worrying that George will be angry and will not
let him raise the rabbits on their farm, he starts to bury it in the hay.
He decides to tell George that he found it dead but then realizes that
George will see through this lie. Frustrated, he curses the dog for
dying and hurls it across the room. Soon, though, Lennie retrieves
the puppy, strokes it again, and reasons that perhaps George won't
care, since the puppy meant nothing to George.

As he talks to himself, Curley's wife enters and sits beside him.
He hastily hides the puppy and tells her that George ordered him not
to speak to her. She reassures him that it is safe for him to talk to her,
pointing out that the other men are occupied with a horseshoe tour-
nament outside and will not interrupt them. She discovers the puppy
and consoles him about its death, declaring that "the whole country
is fulla mutts." She then complains about her loneliness and the cold
treatment she gets from the ranch-hands. She tells Lennie about her
dreams of living a different life. She reveals that her mother denied
her the opportunity to join a traveling show when she was fifteen
and then, years later, a talent scout spotted her and promised to take
her to Hollywood to become a movie star. When nothing came of it,
she decided to marry Curley, whom she dislikes.

Lennie continues to talk about his rabbits, and she asks him why
he likes animals so much. Lennie replies that he likes to touch soft
things with his fingers. She admits that she likes the same thing, and
offers to let him stroke her hair. She warns him not to "muss it," but
he quickly becomes excited and holds on too tight, frightening her.
When she cries out, Lennie panics and clamps his strong hands over
her mouth to silence her. The more she struggles, the tighter his grip
becomes, and he shakes her until her body goes limp. Lennie has
broken her neck.

The barn goes still as Lennie realizes what he has done. He tries
to bury Curley's wife in the hay, worrying chiefly that George will be
angry with him. Taking the puppy's body with him, he flees toward

the meeting place that George designates at the novel's opening—
the clearing in the woods. Candy comes looking for Lennie and
finds the body. He calls George, who realizes immediately what has
happened. George expresses the hope that maybe Lennie will just be
locked up and still be treated well, but Candy tells him that Curley
is sure to have Lennie lynched. Candy asks George if the two of
them can still buy the farm, but sees from George's face that the idea
is now impossible. George says quietly that he thinks he knew all
along that it would never happen, but because Lennie liked the idea
so much, he had started to believe it himself.

George worries that the other men will think that he had something to do with the death of Curley's wife, so he instructs Candy
how to inform them. George will pretend that he has not seen the
body and act surprised when Candy delivers the news. George ex-
its, and Candy curses Curley's wife for destroying their dream of
a farm. After a few moments, his eyes full of tears, he goes to alert
the rest of the ranch. A crowd soon gathers. George comes in last,
with his coat buttoned up. Curley demands that they find Lennie
and kill him. Carlson reports that his gun is missing, and assumes
that Lennie must have taken it. Curley orders them to fetch Crooks's
shotgun, and the mob sets off after Lennie.

ANALYSIS

The scene in the barn begins ominously, with Lennie holding his
puppy, now dead, and stroking it in the same way he stroked the
dead mouse at the beginning of the novel. All sense of optimism for
the farm or the freedom the men would have on it dissolves now that
Lennie's unwittingly dangerous nature has reasserted itself. When
Curley's wife appears and insists on talking with Lennie, the reader
senses that something tragic is about to ensue.

Perhaps the most significant development in this chapter is Steinbeck's depiction of Curley's wife. Before this episode, the reader
might dismiss her as easily as George does. She shows herself to be
a flirt, a conscious temptress, and a manipulator. However, in the
final moments before her death, Steinbeck presents his sole female
character sympathetically. Her loneliness becomes the focus of this
scene, as she admits that she too has an idea of paradise that circumstances have denied her. Her dream of being a movie star is not
unlike George's fantasy of the farm; both are desperately held views
of the way life should be, which have long persisted despite their
conflict with reality.

Curley's wife seems to sense, like Crooks (who notes earlier that Lennie is a good man to talk to), that because Lennie doesn't understand things, a person can say almost anything to him. She confesses her unhappiness in her marriage, her lonely life, and her broken dreams in "a passion of communication." Unfortunately, she fails to see the danger in Lennie, and her attempt to console him for the loss of his puppy by letting him stroke her hair leads to her tragic death. One might take issue with Steinbeck's description of her corpse, for only in her death does he grant her any semblance of virtue. Once she lies lifeless on the hay, Steinbeck writes that all the marks of an unhappy life have disappeared from her face, leaving her looking "pretty and simple . . . sweet and young." The novel has spent considerable time maligning women, and much has been made of their troublesome and seductive natures. It is disturbing, then, that Steinbeck seems to subtly imply that the only way for a woman to overcome that nature and restore her lost innocence is through death.

Lennie's flight from the barn shifts the focus of the narrative to George. As George realizes what Lennie has done, the painful mission that he must undertake becomes clear to him. Here, as in the earlier scene with Candy's dog, Slim becomes the voice of reason, pointing out that the best option for Lennie now is for him to be killed. George understands that he has a choice: either he can watch his friend be murdered by Curley's lynch mob or he can do the deed himself. With this realization, the idea of the farm and the good life it represents disappears. Candy clings to that idealized hope, asking George if they can still buy the farm, but George's response is among the most insightful and realistic responses in the novel. There is no room for dreaming in such a difficult and inhospitable world.

SECTION 6

From Lennie's arrival at the riverbed to the end of the novel

SUMMARY

In the same riverbed where the novel began, it is a beautiful, serene late afternoon. A heron stands in a shaded green pool, eating water snakes that glide between its legs. Lennie comes stealing through the undergrowth and kneels by the water to drink. He is proud of himself for remembering to come here to wait for George, but soon has two unpleasant visions. His Aunt Clara appears "from out of Lennie's head" and berates him, speaking in Lennie's own voice, for not listening to George, for getting himself into trouble, and for causing so many problems for his only friend. Then a gigantic rabbit appears to him, also speaking in Lennie's own voice, and tells him that George will probably beat him and abandon him. Just then, George appears. He is uncommonly quiet and listless. He does not berate Lennie. Even when Lennie himself insists on it, George's tirade is unconvincing and scripted. He repeats his usual words of reproach without emotion. Lennie makes his usual offer to go away and live in a cave, and George tells him to stay, making Lennie feel comforted and hopeful.

Lennie asks him to tell the story of their farm, and George begins, talking about how most men drift along, without any companions, but he and Lennie have one another. The noises of men in the woods come closer, and George tells Lennie to take off his hat and look across the river while he describes their farm. He tells Lennie about the rabbits, and promises that nobody will ever be mean to him again. "Le's do it now," Lennie says. "Le's get that place now." George agrees. He raises Carlson's gun, which he has removed from his jacket, and shoots Lennie in the back of the head. As Lennie falls to the ground and becomes still, George tosses the gun away and sits down on the riverbank.

The sound of the shot brings the lynch party running to the clearing. Carlson questions George, who lets them believe that he wrestled the gun from Lennie and shot him with it. Only Slim understands what really happened: "You hadda, George. I swear you hadda," he tells him. Slim leads George, who is numb with grief, away from the scene, while Carlson and Curley watch incredulously, wondering what is "eatin' them two guys."

ANALYSIS

Once again, the scene opens on the clearing in the woods, with the riverbed and its surroundings described as beautiful and idyllic toward the end of a day. Many details are repeated from the book's opening passages, such as the quality of the sunlight, the distant mountains, and the water snakes with their heads like "periscopes." This time, however, even the natural beauty is marred by the suffering of innocents. Steinbeck vividly describes a large heron bending to snatch an unsuspecting snake out of the water, then waiting as another swims in its direction. Death comes quickly, surely, and to the unaware. When Lennie appears, the fate that awaits him is obvious.

SUMMARY & ANALYSIS

The final scene between George and Lennie is suffused with sadness, even though Lennie retains his blissful ignorance until the end. To reassure Lennie, George forces himself through their habitual interaction one last time. He claims that he is angry, then assures him that all is forgiven and recites the story of their farm. For George, this final description of life with Lennie, of the farm and the changes it would have brought about, is a surrender of his dreams. The vision of the farm recedes, and George realizes that all of his talk and plans have amounted to nothing. He is exactly the kind of man he tried to convince himself he was not, just one among a legion of migrant workers who will never be able to afford more than the occasional prostitute and shot of liquor. Without Lennie, George relinquishes his hope for a different life. Lennie was the only thing that distinguished his life from the lives of other men and gave him a special sense of purpose. With Lennie gone, these hopes cannot be sustained. The grim note on which the novel closes suggests that dreams have no place in a world filled with such injustice and adversity.

The other men who come on the scene see only the body of a half-wit who killed a woman and deserved to die. Only Slim, the wisest and most content man on the ranch, understands George's profound loss and knows that George needs to be consoled. Carlson and Curley watch Slim lead George away from the riverbank; their complete puzzlement is rooted more in ignorance than in heartlessness. Carlson and Curley represent the harsh conditions of a distinctly real world, a world in which the weak will always be vanquished by the strong and in which the rare, delicate bond between friends is not appropriately mourned because it is not understood.

Important Quotations Explained

1. Guys like us, that work on ranches, are the loneliest guys
    in the world. They got no family. They don't belong no
    place. . . . With us it ain't like that. We got a future. We got
    somebody to talk to that gives a damn about us. We don't
    have to sit in no bar room blowin' in our jack jus' because
    we got no place else to go. If them other guys gets in jail
    they can rot for all anybody gives a damn. But not us.

Toward the end of Section 1, before George and Lennie reach the
ranch, they camp for the night in a beautiful clearing and George
assures Lennie of their special relationship. In this passage, George
explains their friendship, which forms the heart of the novel. In
Of Mice and Men, Steinbeck idealizes male friendships, suggesting
that they are the most dignified and satisfying way to overcome the
loneliness that pervades the world.

As a self-declared "watchdog" of society, Steinbeck set out to
expose and chronicle the circumstances that cause human suffering.
Here, George relates that loneliness is responsible for much of that
suffering, a theory supported by many of the secondary characters.
Later in the narrative, Candy, Crooks, and Curley's wife all give
moving speeches about their loneliness and disappointments in life.
Human beings, the novel suggests, are at their best when they have
someone else to look to for guidance and protection. George reminds Lennie that they are extremely lucky to have each other since
most men do not enjoy this comfort, especially men like George and
Lennie, who exist on the margins of society. Their bond is made to
seem especially rare and precious since the majority of the world
does not understand or appreciate it.

At the end, when Lennie accidentally kills Curley's wife, Candy
does not register the tragedy of Lennie's impending death. Instead,
he asks if he and George can still purchase the farm without Lennie.
In this environment, in which human life is utterly disposable, only
Slim recognizes that the loss of such a beautiful and powerful friendship should be mourned.

2.   "S'pose they was a carnival or a circus come to town, or
     a ball game, or any damn thing." Old Candy nodded in
     appreciation of the idea. "We'd just go to her," George
     said. "We wouldn't ask nobody if we could. Jus' say, 'We'll
     go to her,' an' we would. Jus' milk the cow and sling some
     grain to the chickens an' go to her."

In the middle of Section 3, George describes their vision of the farm
to Candy. At first, when Candy overhears George and Lennie discussing the farm they intend to buy, George is guarded, telling the
old man to mind his own business. However, as soon as Candy offers up his life savings for a down payment on the property, George's
vision of the farm becomes even more real.

Described in rustic but lyrical language, the farm is the fuel that
keeps the men going. Life is hard for the men on the ranch and yields
few rewards, but George, Lennie, and now Candy go on because
they believe that one day they will own their own place. The appeal
of this dream rests in the freedom it symbolizes, its escape from
the backbreaking work and spirit-breaking will of others. It pro-
vides comfort from psychological and even physical turmoil, most
obviously for Lennie. For instance, after Curley beats him, Lennie
returns to the idea of tending his rabbits to soothe his pain. Under
their current circumstances, the men must toil to satisfy the boss or
his son, Curley, but they dream of a time when their work will be
easy and determined by themselves only. George's words describe a
timeless, typically American dream of liberty, self-reliance, and the
ability to pursue happiness.

QUOTATIONS

3. A guy sets alone out here at night, maybe readin' books or thinkin' or stuff like that. Sometimes he gets thinkin', an' he got nothing to tell him what's so an' what ain't so. Maybe if he sees somethin', he don't know whether it's right or not. He can't turn to some other guy and ast him if he sees it too. He can't tell. He got nothing to measure by. I seen things out here. I wasn't drunk. I don't know if I was asleep. If some guy was with me, he could tell me I was asleep, an' then it would be all right. But I jus' don't know.

Crooks speaks these words to Lennie in Section 4, on the night that Lennie visits Crooks in his room. The old stable-hand admits to the very loneliness that George describes in the opening pages of the novel. As a black man with a physical handicap, Crooks is forced to live on the periphery of ranch life. He is not even allowed to enter the white men's bunkhouse, or join them in a game of cards. His resentment typically comes out through his bitter, caustic wit, but in this passage he displays a sad, touching vulnerability. Crooks's desire for a friend by whom to "measure" things echoes George's earlier description of the life of a migrant worker. Because these men feel such loneliness, it is not surprising that the promise of a farm of their own and a life filled with strong, brotherly bonds holds such allure.

4.   I seen hundreds of men come by on the road an' on the
       ranches, with their bindles on their back an' that same
       damn thing in their heads . . . every damn one of 'em's got
       a little piece of land in his head. An' never a God damn
       one of 'em ever gets it. Just like heaven. Ever'body wants a
       little piece of lan'. I read plenty of books out here. Nobody
       never gets to heaven, and nobody gets no land.

In this passage from Section 4, after Lennie shares with Crooks his plan to buy a farm with George and raise rabbits, Crooks tries to deflate Lennie's hopes. He relates that "hundreds" of men have passed through the ranch, all of them with dreams similar to Lennie's. Not one of them, he emphasizes with bitterness, ever manages to make that dream come true. Crooks injects the scene with a sense of reality, reminding the reader, if not the childlike Lennie, that the dream of a farm is, after all, only a dream. This moment establishes Crooks's character, showing how a lifetime of loneliness and oppression can manifest as cruelty. It also furthers Steinbeck's disturbing observation that those who have strength and power in the world are not the only ones responsible for oppression. As Crooks shows, even those who are oppressed seek out and attack those who are even weaker than they.

QUOTATIONS

5.   A water snake glided smoothly up the pool, twisting its periscope head from side to side; and it swam the length of the pool and came to the legs of a motionless heron that stood in the shallows. A silent head and beak lanced down and plucked it out by the head, and the beak swallowed the little snake while its tail waved frantically.

The rich imagery with which Steinbeck begins Section 6, the powerful conclusion, evokes the novel's dominant themes. After killing Curley's wife, Lennie returns to the clearing that he and George designate, at the beginning of the novel, as a meeting place should they be separated or run into trouble. Here Steinbeck describes much of the natural splendor as revealed in the opening pages of the novel. The images of the valley and mountains, the climbing sun, and the shaded pool suggest a natural paradise, like the Garden of Eden. The reader's sense of return to a paradise of security and comfort is furthered by the knowledge that George and Lennie have claimed this space as a safe haven, a place to which they can return in times of trouble.

This paradise, however, is lost. The snake sliding through the water recalls the conclusion of the story of Eden, in which the forces of evil appeared as a snake and caused humanity's fall from grace. Steinbeck is a master at symbolism, and here he skillfully employs both the snake and heron to emphasize the predatory nature of the world and to foreshadow Lennie's imminent death. The snake that glides through the waters without harm at the beginning of the novel is now unsuspectingly snatched from the world of the living. Soon, Lennie's life will be taken from him, and he will be just as unsuspecting as the snake when the final blow is delivered.

QUOTATIONS

KEY FACTS

FULL TITLE
Of Mice and Men

AUTHOR
John Steinbeck

TYPE OF WORK
Novel

GENRE
Fiction; tragedy

LANGUAGE
English

TIME AND PLACE WRITTEN
Mid-1930s; Pacific Grove and Los Gatos ranch, California

DATE OF FIRST PUBLICATION
1937

PUBLISHER
Covici, Friede, Inc.

NARRATOR
Third-person omniscient

CLIMAX
Lennie accidentally kills Curley's wife in the barn

PROTAGONISTS
George and Lennie

ANTAGONISTS
Curley; society; the cruel, predatory nature of human life

SETTING (TIME)
1930s

SETTING (PLACE)
South of Soledad, California

POINT OF VIEW

The novel is told from the point of view of a third-person omniscient narrator, who can access the point of view of any character as required by the narrative.

FALLING ACTION

Lennie runs away from the barn; the men return and find Curley's wife dead; Curley leads a mob of men to search for and kill Lennie; George finds Lennie in the clearing and, while retelling the story of life on their farm, shoots him in the back of the head.

TENSE

Past

FORESHADOWING

Lennie petting the dead mouse, Lennie being run out of Weed for the incident involving the girl in the red dress, and Lennie killing his puppy—all of which anticipate Lennie accidentally killing Curley's wife; the death of Candy's dog, which anticipates the death of Lennie; Candy's regret that he didn't kill his old dog himself, which anticipates George's decision to shoot Lennie

TONE

Sentimental, tragic, doomed, fatalistic, rustic, moralistic, comic

THEMES

The predatory nature of human existence; the importance of fraternity and idealized relationships between men; the impossibility of the American Dream; the destructive imbalance of social power structures in American society

MOTIFS

The corrupting power of female sexuality; strength and weakness; loneliness and companionship

SYMBOLS

The clearing in the woods; Lennie and George's farm; mice; Candy's dog; the heron that plucks water snakes from the stream; Curley's boots; Lennie's puppy

KEY FACTS

STUDY QUESTIONS

1. *Discuss the relationship between George and Lennie.*

The friendship that George and Lennie share forms the core of the
novel, and although Steinbeck idealizes and perhaps exaggerates it,
he never questions its sincerity. From Lennie's perspective, George is
the most important person in his life, his guardian and only friend.
Every time he does anything that he knows is wrong, his first thought
is of George's disapproval. He doesn't defend himself from Curley
because of George's stern instruction for him to stay out of trouble,
and when he mistakenly kills his puppy and then Curley's wife, his
only thought is how to quell George's anger. He has a childlike faith
that George will always be there for him, a faith that seems justified,
given their long history together.

George, on the other hand, thinks of Lennie as a constant source
of frustration. He has assumed responsibility for Lennie's welfare
and has, several times, been forced to run because of trouble Lennie
has inadvertently caused. Life with Lennie is not easy. However,
despite George's frequent bouts of anger and frustration, and his
long speeches about how much easier life would be without Lennie,
George is clearly devoted to his friend. He flees from town to town
not to escape the trouble Lennie has caused, but to protect Lennie
from its consequences. The men are uncommonly united by their
shared dream of a better life on a farm where they can "live off
the fatta the lan'," as Lennie puts it. George articulates this vision
by repeatedly telling the "story" of the future farm to his companion. Lennie believes unquestioningly in their dream, and his faith
enables the hardened, cynical George to imagine the possibility of
this dream becoming reality. In fact, George's belief in it depends
upon Lennie, for as soon as Lennie dies, George's hope for a brighter
future disappears.

2. *Discuss the ways in which characters communicate*
    with one another in the novel.

Steinbeck's characters rarely communicate in a straightforward
fashion, often relying on gestures to convey meaning instead. For
example, George does not tell Lennie he loves him, but instead spins
improbable stories about rabbit farms to keep his friend happy.

Curley's wife cannot express how bored she is in her marriage, so she hides from Curley whenever possible and flirts with many of the other men she meets. Candy cannot admit to a sentimental attachment to his aging dog, so he makes excuses or changes the subject when the other men ask him to put the dog out of its misery. The characters let their strongest feelings remain unstated throughout the novel.

The effects of this widespread reticence are tragic. Twice, Steinbeck notes the climate of fear that pervades the novel. (Slim thinks, "Maybe everybody in the whole world is scared of each other," a thought Curley's wife later echoes.) Because George does not try to reason with Curley, he assumes he has to kill Lennie in the story's final moments. Because Curley's wife cannot bare her lonely soul to the men around her, the men persist in believing she is merely a "lousy tart." George never gives voice to his love for Lennie, so Carlson cannot understand why George seems distraught after pulling the trigger. Steinbeck depicts a series of heartbreaking misinterpretations, each the result of the characters' common terror of saying what they're thinking.

3.   *Discuss the role of foreshadowing in the novel.*

Of Mice and Men is an extremely structured work in which each detail anticipates a plot development that follows. Almost every scene points toward the inevitable tragic ending. In the first scene, we learn that Lennie likes to stroke mice and other soft creatures, but has a tendency to kill them accidentally. This foreshadows the death of his puppy and the death of Curley's wife. Furthermore, when George recounts that Lennie once grabbed a woman's dress and would not let go, the reader anticipates that similar trouble will arise at the ranch, especially once Curley's flirtatious wife appears on the scene. Finally, Lennie's panicked but brutal squeezing of Curley's hand anticipates the force with which he grabs Curley's wife by the throat, unintentionally breaking her neck.

The events surrounding Candy's dog, meanwhile, parallel Lennie's fate. Candy is devoted to the animal, just as George is devoted to Lennie, yet the old man must live through the death of his companion, who is shot in the back of the head, just as Lennie is killed at the end of the book. When Candy voices regret that he should have shot his own dog rather than allow Carlson to do it, his words clearly foreshadow the difficult decision that George makes to shoot Lennie rather than leave the deed to Curley's lynch mob. The comparison between the two "gentle animals" is obvious; both are victims of a plot carefully designed for tragedy.

How to Write Literary Analysis

The Literary Essay: A Step-by-Step Guide

When you read for pleasure, your only goal is enjoyment. You might find yourself reading to get caught up in an exciting story, to learn about an interesting time or place, or just to pass time. Maybe you're looking for inspiration, guidance, or a reflection of your own life. There are as many different, valid ways of reading a book as there are books in the world.

When you read a work of literature in an English class, however, you're being asked to read in a special way: you're being asked to perform *literary analysis*. To analyze something means to break it down into smaller parts and then examine how those parts work, both individually and together. Literary analysis involves examining all the parts of a novel, play, short story, or poem—elements such as character, setting, tone, and imagery—and thinking about how the author uses those elements to create certain effects.

A literary essay isn't a book review: you're not being asked whether or not you liked a book or whether you'd recommend it to another reader. A literary essay also isn't like the kind of book report you wrote when you were younger, where your teacher wanted you to summarize the book's action. A high school- or college-level literary essay asks, "How does this piece of literature actually work?" "How does it do what it does?" and, "Why might the author have made the choices he or she did?"

The Seven Steps

No one is born knowing how to analyze literature; it's a skill you learn and a process you can master. As you gain more practice with this kind of thinking and writing, you'll be able to craft a method that works best for you. But until then, here are seven basic steps to writing a well-constructed literary essay:

1. *Ask questions*
2. *Collect evidence*
3. *Construct a thesis*

4. Develop and organize arguments
5. Write the introduction
6. Write the body paragraphs
7. Write the conclusion

---

1. ASK QUESTIONS

When you're assigned a literary essay in class, your teacher will often provide you with a list of writing prompts. Lucky you! Now all you have to do is choose one. Do yourself a favor and pick a topic that interests you. You'll have a much better (not to mention easier) time if you start off with something you enjoy thinking about. If you are asked to come up with a topic by yourself, though, you might start to feel a little panicked. Maybe you have too many ideas—or none at all. Don't worry. Take a deep breath and start by asking yourself these questions:

- **What struck you?** Did a particular image, line, or scene linger in your mind for a long time? If it fascinated you, chances are you can draw on it to write a fascinating essay.

- **What confused you?** Maybe you were surprised to see a character act in a certain way, or maybe you didn't understand why the book ended the way it did. Confusing moments in a work of literature are like a loose thread in a sweater: if you pull on it, you can unravel the entire thing. Ask yourself why the author chose to write about that character or scene the way he or she did and you might tap into some important insights about the work as a whole.

- **Did you notice any patterns?** Is there a phrase that the main character uses constantly or an image that repeats throughout the book? If you can figure out how that pattern weaves through the work and what the significance of that pattern is, you've almost got your entire essay mapped out.

- **Did you notice any contradictions or ironies?** Great works of literature are complex; great literary essays recognize and explain those complexities. Maybe the title (*Happy Days*) totally disagrees with the book's subject matter (hungry orphans dying in the woods). Maybe the main character acts one way around his family and a completely different way around his friends and associates. If you can find a way to explain a work's contradictory elements, you've got the seeds of a great essay.

At this point, you don't need to know exactly what you're going to say about your topic; you just need a place to begin your exploration. You can help direct your reading and brainstorming by formulating your topic as a *question,* which you'll then try to answer in your essay. The best questions invite critical debates and discussions, not just a rehashing of the summary. Remember, you're looking for something you can *prove or argue* based on evidence you find in the text. Finally, remember to keep the scope of your question in mind: is this a topic you can adequately address within the word or page limit you've been given? Conversely, is this a topic big enough to fill the required length?

GOOD QUESTIONS

> *"Are Romeo and Juliet's parents responsible for the deaths of their children?"*
>
> *"Why do pigs keep showing up in* LORD OF THE FLIES*?"*
>
> *"Are Dr. Frankenstein and his monster alike? How?"*

BAD QUESTIONS

> *"What happens to Scout in* TO KILL A MOCKINGBIRD*?"*
>
> *"What do the other characters in* JULIUS CAESAR *think about Caesar?"*
>
> *"How does Hester Prynne in* THE SCARLET LETTER *remind me of my sister?"*

---

2. COLLECT EVIDENCE

Once you know what question you want to answer, it's time to scour the book for things that will help you answer the question. Don't worry if you don't know what you want to say yet—right now you're just collecting ideas and material and letting it all percolate. Keep track of passages, symbols, images, or scenes that deal with your topic. Eventually, you'll start making connections between these examples and your thesis will emerge.

Here's a brief summary of the various parts that compose each and every work of literature. These are the elements that you will analyze in your essay, and which you will offer as evidence to support your arguments. For more on the parts of literary works, see the Glossary of Literary Terms at the end of this section.

ELEMENTS OF STORY   These are the *what*s of the work—what happens, where it happens, and to whom it happens.

- **Plot:** All of the events and actions of the work.
- **Character:** The people who act and are acted upon in a literary work. The main character of a work is known as the *protagonist.*
- **Conflict:** The central tension in the work. In most cases, the protagonist wants something, while opposing forces (antagonists) hinder the protagonist's progress.
- **Setting:** When and where the work takes place. Elements of setting include location, time period, time of day, weather, social atmosphere, and economic conditions.
- **Narrator:** The person telling the story. The narrator may straightforwardly report what happens, convey the subjective opinions and perceptions of one or more characters, or provide commentary and opinion in his or her own voice.
- **Themes:** The main idea or message of the work—usually an abstract idea about people, society, or life in general. A work may have many themes, which may be in tension with one another.

ELEMENTS OF STYLE   These are the *how*s—how the characters speak, how the story is constructed, and how language is used throughout the work.

- **Structure and organization:** How the parts of the work are assembled. Some novels are narrated in a linear, chronological fashion, while others skip around in time. Some plays follow a traditional three- or five-act structure, while others are a series of loosely connected scenes. Some authors deliberately leave gaps in their works, leaving readers to puzzle out the missing information. A work's structure and organization can tell you a lot about the kind of message it wants to convey.
- **Point of view:** The perspective from which a story is told. In *first-person point of view*, the narrator involves him or herself in the story. ("I went to the store"; "We watched in horror as the bird slammed into the window.") A first-person narrator is usually the protagonist of the work, but not always. In *third-person point of view*, the narrator does not participate

in the story. A third-person narrator may closely follow a specific character, recounting that individual character's thoughts or experiences, or it may be what we call an *omniscient* narrator. Omniscient narrators see and know all: they can witness any event in any time or place and are privy to the inner thoughts and feelings of all characters. Remember that the narrator and the author are not the same thing!

- **Diction:** Word choice. Whether a character uses dry, clinical language or flowery prose with lots of exclamation points can tell you a lot about his or her attitude and personality.

- **Syntax:** Word order and sentence construction. Syntax is a crucial part of establishing an author's narrative voice. Ernest Hemingway, for example, is known for writing in very short, straightforward sentences, while James Joyce characteristically wrote in long, incredibly complicated lines.

- **Tone:** The mood or feeling of the text. Diction and syntax often contribute to the tone of a work. A novel written in short, clipped sentences that use small, simple words might feel brusque, cold, or matter-of-fact.

- **Imagery:** Language that appeals to the senses, representing things that can be seen, smelled, heard, tasted, or touched.

- **Figurative language:** Language that is not meant to be interpreted literally. The most common types of figurative language are *metaphors* and *similes,* which compare two unlike things in order to suggest a similarity between them— for example, "All the world's a stage," or "The moon is like a ball of green cheese." (Metaphors say one thing *is* another thing; similes claim that one thing is *like* another thing.)

3. CONSTRUCT A THESIS

When you've examined all the evidence you've collected and know how you want to answer the question, it's time to write your thesis statement. A *thesis* is a claim about a work of literature that needs to be supported by evidence and arguments. The thesis statement is the heart of the literary essay, and the bulk of your paper will be spent trying to prove this claim. A good thesis will be:

- **Arguable.** "*The Great Gatsby* describes New York society in the 1920s" isn't a thesis—it's a fact.

- **Provable through textual evidence**. "*Hamlet* is a confusing but ultimately very well-written play" is a weak thesis because it offers the writer's personal opinion about the book. Yes, it's arguable, but it's not a claim that can be proved or supported with examples taken from the play itself.

- **Surprising**. "Both George and Lenny change a great deal in *Of Mice and Men*" is a weak thesis because it's obvious. A really strong thesis will argue for a reading of the text that is not immediately apparent.

- **Specific**. "Dr. Frankenstein's monster tells us a lot about the human condition" is *almost* a really great thesis statement, but it's still too vague. What does the writer mean by "a lot"? *How* does the monster tell us so much about the human condition?

GOOD THESIS STATEMENTS

Question: In *Romeo and Juliet*, which is more powerful in shaping the lovers' story: fate or foolishness?

Thesis: "Though Shakespeare defines Romeo and Juliet as 'star-crossed lovers' and images of stars and planets appear throughout the play, a closer examination of that celestial imagery reveals that the stars are merely witnesses to the characters' foolish activities and not the causes themselves."

Question: How does the bell jar function as a symbol in Sylvia Plath's *The Bell Jar*?

Thesis: "A bell jar is a bell-shaped glass that has three basic uses: to hold a specimen for observation, to contain gases, and to maintain a vacuum. The bell jar appears in each of these capacities in *The Bell Jar,* Plath's semi-autobiographical novel, and each appearance marks a different stage in Esther's mental breakdown."

Question: Would Piggy in *The Lord of the Flies* make a good island leader if he were given the chance?

Thesis: "Though the intelligent, rational, and innovative Piggy has the mental characteristics of a good leader, he ultimately lacks the social skills necessary to be an effective one. Golding emphasizes this point by giving Piggy a foil in the charismatic Jack, whose magnetic personality allows him to capture and wield power effectively, if not always wisely."

4. DEVELOP AND ORGANIZE ARGUMENTS

The reasons and examples that support your thesis will form the middle paragraphs of your essay. Since you can't really write your thesis statement until you know how you'll structure your argument, you'll probably end up working on steps 3 and 4 at the same time.

There's no single method of argumentation that will work in every context. One essay prompt might ask you to compare and contrast two characters, while another asks you to trace an image through a given work of literature. These questions require different kinds of answers and therefore different kinds of arguments. Below, we'll discuss three common kinds of essay prompts and some strategies for constructing a solid, well-argued case.

TYPES OF LITERARY ESSAYS

- **Compare and contrast**

   Compare and contrast the characters of Huck and Jim in THE ADVENTURES OF HUCKLEBERRY FINN.

   Chances are you've written this kind of essay before. In an academic literary context, you'll organize your arguments the same way you would in any other class. You can either go *subject by subject* or *point by point*. In the former, you'll discuss one character first and then the second. In the latter, you'll choose several traits (attitude toward life, social status, images and metaphors associated with the character) and devote a paragraph to each. You may want to use a mix of these two approaches—for example, you may want to spend a paragraph a piece broadly sketching Huck's and Jim's personalities before transitioning into a paragraph or two that describes a few key points of comparison. This can be a highly effective strategy if you want to make a counterintuitive argument—that, despite seeming to be totally different, the two objects being compared are actually similar in a very important way (or vice versa). Remember that your essay should reveal something fresh or unexpected about the text, so think beyond the obvious parallels and differences.

- **Trace**

   Choose an image—for example, birds, knives, or eyes—and trace that image throughout MACBETH.

   Sounds pretty easy, right? All you need to do is read the play, underline every appearance of a knife in *Macbeth*, and then list them in your essay in the order they appear, right? Well, not exactly. Your teacher doesn't want a simple catalog of examples. He or she wants to see you make *connections* between those examples—that's the difference between summarizing and analyzing. In the *Macbeth* example above, think about the different contexts in which knives appear in the play and to what effect. In *Macbeth,* there are real knives and imagined knives; knives that kill and knives that simply threaten. Categorize and classify your examples to give them some order. Finally, always keep the overall effect in mind. After you choose and analyze your examples, you should come to some greater understanding about the work, as well as your chosen image, symbol, or phrase's role in developing the major themes and stylistic strategies of that work.

- **Debate**

    Is the society depicted in 1984 *good for its citizens?*

    In this kind of essay, you're being asked to debate a moral, ethical, or aesthetic issue regarding the work. You might be asked to judge a character or group of characters (*Is Caesar responsible for his own demise?*) or the work itself (*Is* JANE EYRE *a feminist novel?*). For this kind of essay, there are two important points to keep in mind. First, don't simply base your arguments on your personal feelings and reactions. Every literary essay expects you to read and analyze the work, so search for evidence in the text. What do characters in *1984* have to say about the government of Oceania? What images does Orwell use that might give you a hint about his attitude toward the government? As in any debate, you also need to make sure that you define all the necessary terms before you begin to argue your case. What does it mean to be a "good" society? What makes a novel "feminist"? You should define your terms right up front, in the first paragraph after your introduction.

    Second, remember that strong literary essays make contrary and surprising arguments. Try to think outside the box. In the *1984* example above, it seems like the obvious answer would be no, the totalitarian society depicted in Orwell's novel is *not* good for its citizens. But can you think of any arguments for the opposite side? Even if your final assertion is that the novel depicts a cruel, repressive, and therefore harmful society, acknowledging and responding to the counterargument will strengthen your overall case.

5. WRITE THE INTRODUCTION

Your introduction sets up the entire essay. It's where you present your topic and articulate the particular issues and questions you'll be addressing. It's also where you, as the writer, introduce yourself to your readers. A persuasive literary essay immediately establishes its writer as a knowledgeable, authoritative figure.

An introduction can vary in length depending on the overall length of the essay, but in a traditional five-paragraph essay it should be no longer than one paragraph. However long it is, your introduction needs to:

- **Provide any necessary context.** Your introduction should situate the reader and let him or her know what to expect. What book are you discussing? Which characters? What topic will you be addressing?

- **Answer the "So what?" question.** Why is this topic important, and why is your particular position on the topic noteworthy? Ideally, your introduction should pique the reader's interest by suggesting how your argument is surprising or otherwise counterintuitive. Literary essays make unexpected connections and reveal less-than-obvious truths.

- **Present your thesis.** This usually happens at or very near the end of your introduction.

- **Indicate the shape of the essay to come.** Your reader should finish reading your introduction with a good sense of the scope of your essay as well as the path you'll take toward proving your thesis. You don't need to spell out every step, but you do need to suggest the organizational pattern you'll be using.

Your introduction should not:

- **Be vague.** Beware of the two killer words in literary analysis: *interesting* and *important*. Of course the work, question, or example is interesting and important—that's why you're writing about it!

- **Open with any grandiose assertions.** Many student readers think that beginning their essays with a flamboyant statement such as, "Since the dawn of time, writers have been fascinated with the topic of free will," makes them sound important and commanding. You know what? It actually sounds pretty amateurish.

- **Wildly praise the work.** Another typical mistake student writers make is extolling the work or author. Your teacher doesn't need to be told that "Shakespeare is perhaps the greatest writer in the English language." You can mention a work's reputation in passing—by referring to *The Adventures of Huckleberry Finn* as "Mark Twain's enduring classic," for example—but don't make a point of bringing it up unless that reputation is key to your argument.

- **Go off-topic.** Keep your introduction streamlined and to the point. Don't feel the need to throw in all kinds of bells and whistles in order to impress your reader—just get to the point as quickly as you can, without skimping on any of the required steps.

———————

6. WRITE THE BODY PARAGRAPHS

Once you've written your introduction, you'll take the arguments you developed in step 4 and turn them into your body paragraphs. The organization of this middle section of your essay will largely be determined by the argumentative strategy you use, but no matter how you arrange your thoughts, your body paragraphs need to do the following:

- **Begin with a strong topic sentence.** Topic sentences are like signs on a highway: they tell the reader where they are and where they're going. A good topic sentence not only alerts readers to what issue will be discussed in the following paragraph but also gives them a sense of what argument will be made *about* that issue. "Rumor and gossip play an important role in *The Crucible*" isn't a strong topic sentence because it doesn't tell us very much. "The community's constant gossiping creates an environment that allows false accusations to flourish" is a much stronger topic sentence— it not only tells us *what* the paragraph will discuss (gossip) but *how* the paragraph will discuss the topic (by showing how gossip creates a set of conditions that leads to the play's climactic action).

- **Fully and completely develop a single thought.** Don't skip around in your paragraph or try to stuff in too much material. Body paragraphs are like bricks: each individual

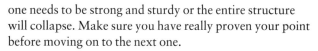

one needs to be strong and sturdy or the entire structure will collapse. Make sure you have really proven your point before moving on to the next one.

- **Use transitions effectively.** Good literary essay writers know that each paragraph must be clearly and strongly linked to the material around it. Think of each paragraph as a response to the one that precedes it. Use transition words and phrases such as *however, similarly, on the contrary, therefore,* and *furthermore* to indicate what kind of response you're making.

---

7. WRITE THE CONCLUSION

Just as you used the introduction to ground your readers in the topic before providing your thesis, you'll use the conclusion to quickly summarize the specifics learned thus far and then hint at the broader implications of your topic. A good conclusion will:

- **Do more than simply restate the thesis.** If your thesis argued that *The Catcher in the Rye* can be read as a Christian allegory, don't simply end your essay by saying, "And that is why *The Catcher in the Rye* can be read as a Christian allegory." If you've constructed your arguments well, this kind of statement will just be redundant.

- **Synthesize the arguments, not summarize them.** Similarly, don't repeat the details of your body paragraphs in your conclusion. The reader has already read your essay, and chances are it's not so long that they've forgotten all your points by now.

- **Revisit the "So what?" question.** In your introduction, you made a case for why your topic and position are important. You should close your essay with the same sort of gesture. What do your readers know now that they didn't know before? How will that knowledge help them better appreciate or understand the work overall?

- **Move from the specific to the general.** Your essay has most likely treated a very specific element of the work—a single character, a small set of images, or a particular passage. In your conclusion, try to show how this narrow discussion has wider implications for the work overall. If your essay on *To Kill a Mockingbird* focused on the character of Boo Radley, for example, you might want to include a bit in your conclusion about how he fits into the novel's larger message about childhood, innocence, or family life.

- **Stay relevant.** Your conclusion should suggest new directions of thought, but it shouldn't be treated as an opportunity to pad your essay with all the extra, interesting ideas you came up with during your brainstorming sessions but couldn't fit into the essay proper. Don't attempt to stuff in unrelated queries or too many abstract thoughts.

- **Avoid making overblown closing statements.** A conclusion should open up your highly specific, focused discussion, but it should do so without drawing a sweeping lesson about life or human nature. Making such observations may be part of the point of reading, but it's almost always a mistake in essays, where these observations tend to sound overly dramatic or simply silly.

A+ Essay Checklist

Congratulations! If you've followed all the steps we've outlined above, you should have a solid literary essay to show for all your efforts. What if you've got your sights set on an A+? To write the kind of superlative essay that will be rewarded with a perfect grade, keep the following rubric in mind. These are the qualities that teachers expect to see in a truly A+ essay. How does yours stack up?

- ✓ Demonstrates a thorough understanding of the book
- ✓ Presents an original, compelling argument
- ✓ Thoughtfully analyzes the text's formal elements
- ✓ Uses appropriate and insightful examples
- ✓ Structures ideas in a logical and progressive order
- ✓ Demonstrates a mastery of sentence construction, transitions, grammar, spelling, and word choice

Suggested Essay Topics

1. *Discuss the novel's view of relationships between men.*

2. *Analyze Steinbeck's portrayal of Curley's wife as the lone female on the all-male ranch.*

3. *Paying attention to the long descriptive passages at the beginning of each section, discuss the ways in which the novel is similar to a theatrical play. Do these similarities strengthen or weaken the novel? How?*

4. *Discuss George's actions at the end of the novel. How can we justify what he does to Lennie? How can we condemn it?*

5. *Discuss Steinbeck's descriptions of the natural world. What role does nature play in the novel's symbolism?*

6. *Analyze the characters of Slim, Crooks, and Curley. What role does each character play?*

A+ STUDENT ESSAY

> Discuss the role of dreams in *Of Mice and Men.* What
> purpose do they serve? Are they ultimately beneficial or
> harmful?

In *Of Mice and Men,* it seems an incontrovertible law of nature
that dreams should go unfulfilled. From George and Lennie's ranch
to Curley's wife's stardom, the characters' most cherished aspira-
tions repeatedly fail to materialize. However, the fact that they *do*
dream—often long after the possibility of realizing those dreams
has vanished—suggests that dreaming serves a purpose in their
lives. What the characters ultimately fail to see is that, in Steinbeck's
harsh world, dreams are not only a source of happiness but a source
of misery as well.

For the characters in *Of Mice and Men,* dreams are useful
because they map out the possibilities of human happiness. Just as
a map helps a traveler locate himself on the road, dreams help Lennie, George, and the others understand where they are and where
they're going. Many dreams in the novel have a physical dimension:
Not just wishes to be achieved, they are places to be reached. The
fact that George's ranch, the central dream of the novel, is an actual
place as opposed to a person or a thing underlines this geographical
element. Dreams turn the characters' otherwise meandering lives
into journeys with a purpose, as they take pride in actions that support the achievement of their dreams and reject actions that do not.
Having a destination gives the men's lives meaning. Indeed, when
others begin to believe in the dream-space that George has created,
it becomes almost realer to them than the farm they work at, a phe-
nomenon illustrated by Candy's constant "figuring" about how to
make good on their fantasy.

Dreams help the characters feel like more active participants in
their own lives because they allow them to believe that the choices
they make can have real, tangible benefits. They also help characters
cope with misery and hardship, keeping them from succumbing to
the difficulties they face regularly. In their darkest moments, George
and Lennie invoke their ranch like a spell that can temper their daily
sufferings and injustices. George and Lennie almost always fanta-
size about the ranch after some traumatic event or at the end of
a long day, suggesting that they rely on their dreams as a kind of

salve. The dream of the ranch offers George, Lennie, Candy, and the others a goal to work toward as well as the inspiration to keep struggling when things seem grim.

But by the end of the story, Steinbeck reveals that dreams can be as poisonous as they are beneficial. What George discovers—and what Crooks already seems to know when he scornfully spurns Candy's offer to join him, Lennie, and George—is that dreams are too often merely an articulation of what never can be. In such cases, dreams become a source of intense bitterness because they seduce cynical men to believe in them and then mock those men for their gullibility. The workers' love of Western magazines suggests just such a relationship to dreams: Each one scoffs at the magazines in public but manages to sneak furtive glances when no one else is looking, as if they secretly wanted to be the cowboy heroes of pulp fiction. No one seems to understand this bitterness better than Crooks, whose sullen self-loathing is never stronger than when he lets himself believe in Lennie's dream, only to be brutally reminded by Curley's wife that he is not entitled to happiness in a white man's world.

Ultimately, the dreams of ranches and rabbits that George and Lennie treasure are the very things that undo them. Seduced by how close he thinks he is to realizing his dream, George fools himself into thinking that Lennie can mind himself and stay out of trouble when past events confirm the contrary. In the end, George does not despair at Lennie's death because the ranch is forever lost to him, but rather because his friend—the one good reality of his life, the one reality that redeemed George from worthlessness—is forever lost to him.

GLOSSARY OF LITERARY TERMS

ANTAGONIST

The entity that acts to frustrate the goals of the *protagonist*. The antagonist is usually another *character* but may also be a non-human force.

ANTIHERO / ANTIHEROINE

A *protagonist* who is not admirable or who challenges notions of what should be considered admirable.

CHARACTER

A person, animal, or any other thing with a personality that appears in a *narrative*.

CLIMAX

The moment of greatest intensity in a text or the major turning point in the *plot*.

CONFLICT

The central struggle that moves the *plot* forward. The conflict can be the *protagonist*'s struggle against fate, nature, society, or another person.

FIRST-PERSON POINT OF VIEW

A literary style in which the *narrator* tells the story from his or her own *point of view* and refers to himself or herself as "I." The narrator may be an active participant in the story or just an observer.

HERO / HEROINE

The principal *character* in a literary work or *narrative*.

IMAGERY

Language that brings to mind sense-impressions, representing things that can be seen, smelled, heard, tasted, or touched.

MOTIF

A recurring idea, structure, contrast, or device that develops or informs the major *themes* of a work of literature.

NARRATIVE

A story.

NARRATOR

The person (sometimes a *character*) who tells a story; the *voice* assumed by the writer. The narrator and the author of the work of literature are not the same person.

PLOT

The arrangement of the events in a story, including the sequence in which they are told, the relative emphasis they are given, and the causal connections between events.

POINT OF VIEW

The *perspective* that a *narrative* takes toward the events it describes.

PROTAGONIST

The main *character* around whom the story revolves.

SETTING

The location of a *narrative* in time and space. Setting creates mood or atmosphere.

SUBPLOT

A secondary *plot* that is of less importance to the overall story but may serve as a point of contrast or comparison to the main plot.

SYMBOL

An object, *character,* figure, or color that is used to represent an abstract idea or concept. Unlike an *emblem,* a symbol may have different meanings in different contexts.

SYNTAX

The way the words in a piece of writing are put together to form lines, phrases, or clauses; the basic structure of a piece of writing.

THEME

A fundamental and universal idea explored in a literary work.

TONE

The author's attitude toward the subject or *characters* of a story or poem or toward the reader.

VOICE

An author's individual way of using language to reflect his or her own personality and attitudes. An author communicates voice through *tone, diction,* and *syntax.*

LITERARY ANALYSIS

A NOTE ON PLAGIARISM

Plagiarism—presenting someone else's work as your own—rears its ugly head in many forms. Many students know that copying text without citing it is unacceptable. But some don't realize that even if you're not quoting directly, but instead are paraphrasing or summarizing, *it is plagiarism* unless you cite the source.

Here are the most common forms of plagiarism:

- Using an author's phrases, sentences, or paragraphs without citing the source
- Paraphrasing an author's ideas without citing the source
- Passing off another student's work as your own

How do you steer clear of plagiarism? You should *always* acknowledge all words and ideas that aren't your own by using quotation marks around verbatim text or citations like footnotes and endnotes to note another writer's ideas. For more information on how to give credit when credit is due, ask your teacher for guidance or visit www.sparknotes.com.

REVIEW & RESOURCES

QUIZ

1. *Of Mice and Men* was first published in what year?

   A. 1919
   B. 1962
   C. 1937
   D. 1939

2. What is the name of the town from which George and Lennie are fleeing when the novel opens?

   A. Weed
   B. Soledad
   C. Salinas
   D. The town is never named.

3. What excites Lennie most about his dream life with George?

   A. He will learn to farm.
   B. He will get to tend rabbits.
   C. They will both find "purty" girls and settle down.
   D. He will strike it rich panning for gold.

4. Why is Candy unable to imagine getting rid of his old dog?

   A. The dog is a fine watchdog.
   B. He makes too much money breeding the animal.
   C. He promised his wife on her deathbed that he would care for it.
   D. He has had the dog since it was a puppy.

5. Why does Curley wear a Vaseline-filled glove on one hand?

   A. He wants to keep his hand soft for his wife.
   B. His hand was mangled in a piece of farm equipment.
   C. He is soothing an old boxing injury.
   D. He is incredibly vain.

6.   Why does Carlson insist on shooting Candy's dog?

    A.   The dog has attacked several people.
    B.   Carlson is mean-spirited and drunk.
    C.   Carlson believes the dog is too old and decrepit to be of any use.
    D.   Carlson hates dogs.

7.   Whit enters the bunkhouse with a magazine featuring a man he used to work with. Why is the man in the magazine?

    A.   He wrote a letter to the editor, praising the publication.
    B.   He was an undercover journalist, who wrote a piece exposing the difficult working conditions of migrant farmers.
    C.   He is a fugitive, the subject of a nationwide manhunt.
    D.   He recently bought a farm much like the one George and Lennie hope to own.

8.   What is Old Susy's place?

    A.   A restaurant
    B.   A saloon
    C.   George's mother's home
    D.   A flophouse

9.   Who discovers Curley's dead wife?

    A.   George
    B.   Curley
    C.   Candy
    D.   Carlson

10.   What does Curley wear to set himself apart from the other men?

    A.   A denim jacket
    B.   High-heeled boots
    C.   A bull whip
    D.   Gloves

11. Who cared for Lennie before George?

    A. Lennie's aunt Clara
    B. Lennie's mother
    C. George's aunt Clara
    D. George's mother

12. *Of Mice and Men* is set in which decade?

    A. 1910s
    B. 1920s
    C. 1930s
    D. 1940s

13. What does Curley's wife offer to let Lennie touch?

    A. Her dress
    B. Her face
    C. Her hand
    D. Her hair

14. To whom does Candy look for advice before allowing Carlson to shoot his dog?

    A. Lennie
    B. Crooks
    C. Slim
    D. The boss

15. Why do many critics find fault with *Of Mice and Men*?

    A. They believe that the novel is too short.
    B. They find Steinbeck's portrayal of Lennie excessively sentimental.
    C. They wish that the novel had a happy ending.
    D. They believe that the novel does not accurately depict life during the Depression.

16. How does Steinbeck foreshadow the death of Curley's wife?

   A.   He dresses the woman in fancy red shoes.
   B.   He opens the chapter in which she dies with Lennie petting his dead puppy.
   C.   He gives her a moving speech in which she admits her dream of being a movie star.
   D.   He points out several times that Lennie doesn't like her.

17. How did Crooks get his name?

   A.   He was born with it.
   B.   He has a crooked back.
   C.   He served time in jail for robbery.
   D.   He has a crooked smile.

18. Before George meets Lennie in the woods in the final scene, whose gun does he take?

   A.   Carlson's
   B.   Slim's
   C.   Curley's
   D.   Candy's

19. What does George say to Lennie before shooting him?

   A.   He tells Lennie that he is a bad man and that he deserves to die.
   B.   He tells Lennie that he has no other choice but to shoot him since it's the law.
   C.   He tells Lennie the story of their farm.
   D.   He tells Lennie he's sorry that he let him down.

20. When Lennie drops down next to the pool of water as the novel opens, what is George's advice to him?

    A.   He tells him to drink up now, because there's no telling when they'll find water again.

    B.   He tells him to bathe.

    C.   He tells him to wash his hands after playing with the dead mouse.

    D.   He tells him not to drink too much water to avoid getting sick.

21. Who is the only man to understand the bond between Lennie and George?

    A.   Crooks

    B.   Curley

    C.   Slim

    D.   None of the men understand their bond.

22. After killing Curley's wife, which of the following pairs does Lennie imagine appears to chastise his behavior?

    A.   Aunt Clara and his mother

    B.   Aunt Clara and a giant rabbit

    C.   George and Curley

    D.   George and Curley's wife

23. Whom do Lennie and George agree to let live on their farm?

    A.   Candy

    B.   Curley's wife

    C.   Old Susy

    D.   Slim

24. Why doesn't Crooks allow Lennie to enter his room at first?

   A. Because Lennie isn't much of a conversationalist and Crooks enjoys talking long into the night
   B. Because he fears Lennie's strength
   C. Because he says a white man shouldn't be allowed in his room since he is not allowed in the white men's bunkhouse
   D. Because he prefers to keep to himself

25. Disappointed with her life, Curley's wife wonders where she would be if she had followed her dreams and become which of the following things?

   A. A movie star
   B. A schoolteacher
   C. A showgirl
   D. A nurse

Suggestions for Further Reading

BLOOM, HAROLD. *John Steinbeck's* OF MICE AND MEN. New York: Chelsea House Publishers, 1999.

GEORGE, STEPHEN K. *The Moral Philosophy of John Steinbeck.* Lanham, MD: Scarecrow Press, Inc., 2005.

HADELLA, CHARLOTTE. OF MICE AND MEN: *A Kinship of Powerlessness.* New York: Twayne Publishers, 1995.

HARMON, ROBERT B. *Steinbeck Bibliographies: An Annotated Guide.* Metuchen, NJ: Scarecrow Press, 1987.

HAYASHI, TETSUMARO, ed. *John Steinbeck: The Years of Greatness, 1936–1939.* Tuscaloosa: University of Alabama Press, 1993.

MEYER, MICHAEL J. *The Betrayal of Brotherhood in the Work of John Steinbeck.* Lewiston, NY: Edwin Mellen Press, 2000.

PARINI, JAY. *John Steinbeck: A Biography.* London: Heinemann, 1994.

SCHULTZ, JEFFREY. *Critical Companion to John Steinbeck: A Literary Reference to His Life and Work.* New York: Checkmark Books, 2005.

SIMMONDS, ROY S. *A Biographical and Critical Introduction of John Steinbeck.* Lewiston, NY: Edwin Mellen Press, 2000.

ST. PIERRE, BRIAN. *John Steinbeck, The California Years.* San Francisco: Chronicle Books, 1983.

SWISHER, CLARICE, ed. *Readings on John Steinbeck.* San Diego: Greenhaven Press, 1996.

REVIEW & RESOURCES

SparkNotes Literature Guides

1984

The Adventures of
Huckleberry Finn

The Adventures of
Tom Sawyer

The Aeneid

All Quiet on the
Western Front

And Then There Were
None

Angela's Ashes

Animal Farm

Anna Karenina

Anne of Green Gables

Anthem

As I Lay Dying

The Awakening

The Bean Trees

Beloved

Beowulf

Billy Budd

Black Boy

Bless Me, Ultima

The Bluest Eye

Brave New World

The Brothers
Karamazov

The Call of the Wild

Candide

The Canterbury Tales

Catch-22

The Catcher in the Rye

The Chocolate War

The Chosen

Cold Sassy Tree

The Color Purple

The Count of Monte
Cristo

Crime and Punishment

The Crucible

Cry, the Beloved
Country

Cyrano de Bergerac

David Copperfield

Death of a Salesman

Death of Socrates

Diary of a Young Girl

A Doll's House

Don Quixote

Dr. Faustus

Dr. Jekyll and Mr. Hyde

Dracula

Edith Hamilton's
Mythology

Emma

Ethan Frome

Fahrenheit 451

A Farewell to Arms

The Fellowship of the
Rings

Flowers for Algernon

For Whom the Bell
Tolls

The Fountainhead

Frankenstein

The Giver

The Glass Menagerie

The Good Earth

The Grapes of Wrath

Great Expectations

The Great Gatsby

Grendel

Gulliver's Travels

Hamlet

The Handmaid's Tale

Hard Times

Heart of Darkness

Henry IV, Part I

Henry V

Hiroshima

The Hobbit

The House on Mango
Street

I Know Why the Caged
Bird Sings

The Iliad

The Importance of
Being Earnest

Inferno

Invisible Man

Jane Eyre

Johnny Tremain

The Joy Luck Club

Julius Caesar

The Jungle

The Killer Angels

King Lear

The Last of the
Mohicans

Les Misérables

A Lesson Before Dying

Little Women

Lord of the Flies

Macbeth

Madame Bovary

The Merchant of
Venice

A Midsummer Night's
Dream

Moby-Dick

Much Ado About
Nothing

My Ántonia

Narrative of the Life of
Frederick Douglass

Native Son

The New Testament

Night

The Odyssey

Oedipus Plays

Of Mice and Men

The Old Man and
the Sea

The Old Testament

Oliver Twist

The Once and Future
King

One Flew Over the
Cuckoo's Nest

One Hundred Years of
Solitude

Othello

Our Town

The Outsiders

Paradise Lost

The Pearl

The Picture of Dorian
Gray

Poe's Short Stories

A Portrait of the Artist
as a Young Man

Pride and Prejudice

The Prince

A Raisin in the Sun

The Red Badge of
Courage

The Republic

The Return of the King

Richard III

Robinson Crusoe

Romeo and Juliet

Scarlet Letter

A Separate Peace

Silas Marner

Sir Gawain and the
Green Knight

Slaughterhouse-Five

Song of Solomon

The Sound and the
Fury

The Stranger

A Streetcar Named
Desire

The Sun Also Rises

A Tale of Two Cities

The Taming of the
Shrew

The Tempest

Tess of the
d'Urbervilles

The Things They
Carried

The Two Towers

Their Eyes Were
Watching God

Things Fall Apart

To Kill a Mockingbird

Treasure Island

Twelfth Night

Ulysses

Uncle Tom's Cabin

Walden

War and Peace

Wuthering Heights

A Yellow Raft in Blue
Water

Visit sparknotes.com for many more!